COMMUNIST EXPLOITATION OF RELIGION

HEARING

BEFORE THE

SUBCOMMITTEE TO INVESTIGATE THE ADMINISTRATION OF THE INTERNAL SECURITY ACT AND OTHER INTERNAL SECURITY LAWS

OF THE

COMMITTEE ON THE JUDICIARY UNITED STATES SENATE

EIGHTY-NINTH CONGRESS

TESTIMONY OF REV. RICHARD WURMBRAND

MAY 6, 1966

Printed for the use of the Committee on the Judiciary

COMMUNIST EXPLOITATION OF RELIGION

ISBN   0-88264-068-2

Copyright ⓒ1982 By Diane Books Publishing Co.
Printed in U.S.A.

COMMUNIST EXPLOITATION OF RELIGION

FRIDAY, MAY 6, 1966

U.S. Senate,
Subcommittee To Investigate the
Administration of the Internal Security Act
and Other Internal Security Laws,
of the Committee on the Judiciary,
Washington, D.C.

The subcommittee met, pursuant to call, at 10:20 a.m., in room 318, Old Senate Office Building, Senator Thomas J. Dodd presiding.

Also present: Jay G. Sourwine, chief counsel; Benjamin Mandel, director of research; Frank W. Schroeder, chief investigator; and Robert C. McManus, investigations analyst.

Senator Dodd. I will call this hearing to order. We have as our witness today Pastor Richard Wurmbrand, who is a refugee from Rumania. Mr. Sourwine will introduce and read a copy of Dr. Wurmbrand's credentials.

I must say, before you do so, that we are grateful for your appearing here. I am familiar with the nature of your testimony—I think I am—to an extent. I feel that you are rendering a real service to the cause of the free world.

Go ahead, Mr. Sourwine.

Mr. Sourwine. Mr. Chairman, this letter of credentials, which I shall read pursuant to your instructions, was given to Dr. Wurmbrand by Dr. Hedenquist, who is the mission director of the Svenska Israelsmissionen. The reason is explained in the text. It reads:

Pastor Richard Wurmbrand is a refugee from Rumania, a country which he had to leave because of the antireligious persecution. Fleeing from there, he has not the usual credentials, which have been taken from him at his arrestation by the secret police of the Communists.

Our mission, knowing him since 26 years, certify hereby that he is an Evangelical Minister who has had until now the following functions:

From April 1939, to January 1940, he was secretary of the church's mission to the Jews which had to retire from Rumania at the last date because of the war.

During the whole war he has been pastor of our mission in Rumania.

Since our mission retired from Rumania in 1945, from that year to 1948 he has been a pastor of the Norwegian mission to the Jews.

In the same time he has worked also in the representation of the World Council of Churches for Rumania.

He was also a professor of the Old Testament in the Seminary of Bucharest.

From 1948 to 1956, he was in prison for religious motives.

Released in 1956, he was no more authorized by the Communist authorities to fulfill his duties. From 1956 to 1959 he preached and exercised his other pastoral functions illegally.

Rearrested for this in 1959, he was again in prison until July 1964, when he was released on the basis of a general amnesty.

Since 1964, he was pastor of the Evangelical Church in Orshova, a Rumanian town.

1

Continuing to be the object of persecution and being in great danger, our Scandinavian missions to the Jews succeeded to make him escape from there.

We recommend him as a most reliable person, a fine Christian who has published several books against atheism and communism and who has got a burning heart for Christ and for all people in need.

This is signed by Dr. Hedenquist, doctor of theology, mission director in Sweden for Svenska Israelsmissionen.

Reverand WURMBRAND. He is the former secretary of the World Council of Missions.

Senator DODD. Without objection, this letter will be included in the record. Since it has been read, it will not be reprinted.

Mr. Sourwine, you may proceed. I have some questions which I might as well ask to begin with, rather than wait until later.

Pastor, how many languages do you speak?

Reverend WURMBRAND. There are legends about me that I speak very many languages. Something like 14.

Senator DODD. Forty?

Reverend WURMBRAND. Fourteen.

Senator DODD. Obviously, you speak English.

Reverend WURMBRAND. Yes; English, French, German, Hungarian, and so on.

Senator DODD. Did you come directly from Rumania?

Reverend WURMBRAND. No, no; from Rumania I went to Italy, from Italy to Oslo, and then from Europe I came to the States.

Senator DODD. From where?

Reverend WURMBRAND. From Paris.

Senator DODD. When was that?

Reverend WURMBRAND. I came to the States 3 weeks ago.

Senator DODD. Were you required by the secret police to make any commitments before you could leave Rumania?

Reverend WURMBRAND. Before I left Rumania I was called twice to the secret police. The first time they said that they don't know yet if they will allow me to leave the country with my family. They said: "Dollars have been received for you. You will have to leave the country, but perhaps we will let some time to pass, because your remembrances of prison are too fresh and you have too good a pen."

Senator DODD. What?

Reverend WURMBRAND. A pen. "You can too well write. Perhaps we will keep somebody here of your family as hostage."

The second time they called me again and they said: "Now you will leave the country, but be very cautious when you come out. You may preach Christ as much as you like. We know that you are a preacher, but don't touch us. Don't speak against Communists. If you will speak against communism, for $1,000 we can find a gangster who will liquidate you. We play with you with open cards. You come from prison. You have met in prison men whom we have brought back from the West."

And that is the truth. I have been in prison with a Rumanian Orthodox priest, Vasile Leul, who has been kidnaped from Austria. I have seen his nails torn out and broken, and so they reminded me of that. "You know how our prisons are and that you can come back in prison."

And the third thing which they said: "We have also another possibility with you. We can destroy you morally outside. We will find a story with a girl or a money story or something else and people will be stupid enough to believe it. We will destroy you if you touch us."

And under these conditions I was allowed to come out. And very sorrowfully in the West I found people in the West, even religious leaders, who told me the same thing: "Preach Christ as much as you like but don't touch Communists."

Senator DODD. As I understand it, you said you came to this country 3 weeks ago.

Reverend WURMBRAND. Yes, sir; just today it is 1 month.

Senator DODD. Three weeks?

Reverend WURMBRAND. One month today.

Senator DODD. Were you in prison from 1948 to 1956?

Reverend WURMBRAND. Yes, and then imprisoned again in January 1959 to 1964.

Senator DODD. Were you in the same prison all of that time?

Reverend WURMBRAND. No, no; we were transferred from one prison to the others.

Senator DODD. From 1956 to 1959 as I understand it, you exercised your religious function in spite of the law against such activity, did you not?

Reverend WURMBRAND. Yes, yes.

Senator DODD. How did you do this?

Reverend WURMBRAND. When I came out from prison in 1956, I was licensed to preach—of course, nobody can preach in our country except he has a license from the Government—and in the beginning I got a license, but which was withdrawn from me after the first week of preaching.

The motives are so comical you would say. In a sermon I said that Christians must keep hope, because the wheel of history turns, and the wheel of life.

"You meant us, that communism will change, that communism will fall. Never will it fall." It has been reproached to me that in a sermon I have said Christians must practice patience, patience, and again patience. "Ah, you meant that the Americans will come and we must be patient until they come."

Everything was misinterpreted, and so the license has been withdrawn from me. And then generally in the Soviet countries there exists the underground church which works as the first Christians worked. Only now we understand texts of the Bible which we had not understood before. I did not know why it is written in the Bible that a man named Simon was called Peter. Simeon was called Niger and so on. Everyone is called otherwise than his mother called him. So it is with us now. In every village I was called by another name. I was called Valentin, Georgescu, Ruben. In every village I had another name, and so I could preach.

I did not understand in earlier times why Jesus, when He wishes to have the last supper, said: "Go in town and you will see a man with a pitcher and go after him and where he enters prepare the supper."

Why does he not give an address, a number, and a street? Now we know it when we make secret prayer meetings. We never give the address. We don't know if that man is not the informer of the secret police. We tell to the man to wait in a public garden or somewhere, and when one with a flower here, or with a necktie passes, go after him. We don't introduce ourselves to each other, and if somebody asks the name of the other one, we know that he is the informer of the secret police. And so we have developed a technique of secret church work, and so I could work.

Senator Dodd. How did you keep alive? How did you sustain yourself?

Reverend Wurmbrand. The Christians sustained me everywhere. I had no salary, I had no regular salary but the Christians everywhere sustained me. In Rumania the first question asked about a pastor or a priest of any denomination, is: Has he been in prison? If he has been in prison he is all right. All the Christians sustain him.

Senator Dodd. You were rearrested in 1959, as I understand it.

Reverend Wurmbrand. Yes.

Senator Dodd. Were you kept in the same prison until your release in 1964?

Reverend Wurmbrand. No. Then, also, I was in several prisons.

Senator Dodd. Could you describe for us the cell in which you were kept in solitary confinement?

Reverend Wurmbrand. There were different cells. In solitary confinement I was the first 2½, nearly 3 years. It was in the most beautiful building of Bucharest in the building of the Secretariat of State for Internal Affairs. It is a building before which all foreigners stand and admire it. I can tell you that your White House is a very little building in comparison with ours. And there beneath the earth, 10 meters beneath the earth are the cells. There are no windows in the cells. Air enters through a tube. And there were a few desks, with a mattress, with a straw mattress. You had but three steps for a walk. Never were we taken out from these cells except for interrogations when prisoners were beaten and tortured.

For years I have never seen sun, moon, flowers, snow, stars, no man except the interrogator who beat, but I can say I have seen heaven open, I have seen Jesus Christ, I have seen the angels and we were very happy there.

But the treatment was very bad. The purpose was to make us mad. You didn't hear a noise. A whisper you didn't hear in this cell. The guard had felt shoes. For years, not to hear anything. In all these years of prison we never had a book, we never had a bit of paper, we never had a newspaper, nothing to distract our mind except that from time to time tape recorders were put on the corridor. I didn't know what a tape recorder is. I had not seen such a thing. But at once we heard beautiful Rumanian music, and then we enjoyed it. We didn't know what has happened with the Communists that they make us enjoy, and after 10 or 15 minutes at once you heard, "Ha, ha, ha, don't beat," the torturing of a woman. This lasted for half an hour, the torturing of a woman. And of 100 prisoners who had been in that cell, in that corridor, everybody recognized that it is his wife or that it is his girl. I myself thought also that it is my wife.

Never will a Westerner understand, if I would not have the marks on my body, which are my credentials.

Senator Dodd. Excuse me, never will who understand?

Reverend Wurmbrand. A Westerner can't understand.

Senator Dodd. A Westerner?

Reverend Wurmbrand. A Westerner can't understand God is here and knows that I will not tell you the whole truth because if I will tell you the whole truth, you will faint and rush out of this room, not bearing to hear what things have happened. But I will tell you that in a prison they crucified a cat before ourselves. They beat nails in the feet of the cat and the cat was hanging with the head down, and now you imagine how this cat screamed and the prisoners, mad, beat on the door, "Free the cat, free the cat, free the cat," and the Communists very polite, "Oh, surely we will free the cat, but give the statements which we ask from you and then the cat will be freed," and I have known men who have given statements against their wives, against their children, against their parents to free the cat. They did it out of madness, and then the parents and the wives have been tortured like the cat. Such things have happened with us.

Senator DODD. Did you have any fellow Christian like you imprisoned?

Reverend WURMBRAND. We had hundreds of bishops, priests, monks in prisons; my wife who is near me, she has been with Catholic nuns. My wife tells that they were angels; such have been put in prisons. Nearly all Catholic bishops died in prison. Innumerable Orthodox and Protestants have been in prison, too.

Senator DODD. The point I was getting at—and I guess I did not make it clear—were the Christians treated any differently or mistreated any differently?

Reverend WURMBRAND. Everybody in prison was very badly treated. And I cannot be contradicted on this question, because I have been with physicians, I have much more broken bones than anybody, so either I broke my bones or somebody else broke them. And if I would not have been a clergyman but a murderer—it is a crime to torture a murderer, too. The Christian prisoners were tortured in a form which should mock their religion. I tell you again in the prison of Pitesti one scene I will describe you about torturing and mocking Christians, and believe me I would renounce to eternal life to paradise after which I long, if I tell you one word of exaggeration. God is here and knows that I do not say everything. It cannot be said. There are ladies here. There are other people hearing it.

One Sunday morning in the prison of Pitesti a young Christian was already the fourth day, day and night, tied to the cross. Twice a day the cross was put on the floor and 100 other cell inmates by beating, by tortures, were obliged to fulfill their necessities upon his face and upon his body. Then the cross was erected again and the Communists swearing and mocking "Look your Christ, look your Christ, how beautiful he is, adore him, kneel before him, how fine he smells, your Christ." And then the Sunday morning came and a Catholic priest, an acquaintance of mine, has been put to the belt, in the dirt of a cell with 100 prisoners, a plate with excrements, and one with urine was given to him and he was obliged to say the holy mass upon these elements, and he did it. And I asked him afterward, "Father, but how could you make this?" He was half mad. He answered to me: "Brother, I have suffered more than Christ. Don't reproach to me what I have done." And the other prisoners beaten to take holy communion in this form, and the Communists around, "Look, your sacraments, look, your church, what a holy church you have, what fine is your church, what holy ordinance God has given you."

I am a very insignificant and a very little man. I have been in prison among the weak ones and the little ones, but I speak for a suffering country and for a suffering church and for the heroes and the saints of the 20th century; we have had such saints in our prison to which I did not dare to lift my eyes.

I am a Protestant, but we have had near us Catholic bishops and monks and nuns about whom we felt that the touching of their garments heals. We were not worthy to untie their shoelaces. Such men have been mocked and tortured in our country. And even if it would mean to go back to a Rumanian prison, to be kidnaped by the Communists and going back and tortured again, I cannot be quiet. I owe it to those who have suffered there.

Senator DODD. Now, did the Rumanian secret police employ brain-washing techniques?

Reverend WURMBRAND. The worst thing has been the brainwashing. All the tortures of times before were nothing in comparison with brainwashing.

To describe very shortly brainwashing: First of all we were doped. The dope was put in our food. I did not know about this dope. But we saw only the results, a dope which gave two results. First of all, what the physician calls aleulia which means lack of power of will. The power of will was completely broken. If we were told, "Lift your hand," I lifted it. If I was not told to let the hand down, I would never have left it down. We were at the same time very much undernourished. We had times when we received 100 grams, one slice of bread, a week. It was told to us, "We give you as many calories as you need to be able to breathe only," and so our power of will has been broken.

Second, this drug or perhaps it is another drug, produces the delirium of self-accusation. I have seen prisoners knocking during the night on the door and saying, "Take me to the interrogator, I have new things to say against me." Prisoners quarreled with their interrogators to say against themselves more than the interrogators asked from them. And then we have had in prisons the curious phenomenon that we as priests received confessions from other prisoners. Now everybody is a sinner, but not everybody is a criminal. Men who have never murdered confessed that they have murdered, that they have committed adultery, that they have stolen. They felt they had to accuse themselves. This has also been the result of this doping. And after we were doped like that—that is the secret of all the Soviet show trials, in which the prisoners accuse themselves— then the time of brainwashing came. For 17 hours a day from 5 in the morning to 10 in the evening we had to sit like this. We were not allowed to lean. We were not allowed to rest a little bit our weary heads upon our hands. To close your eyes was a crime. Seventeen hours a day we had to sit like that and hear from the morning to the evening: "Communism is good, communism is good, communism is good, communism is good," until you heard one who was already 20 years in prison under the Communists shouting, "Communism is good, communism is good, communism is good, I give my life for communism."

It was after the technique of Professor Pavlov, a scientifical suggestion.

In prison there were not only priests and pastors. We have had hundreds of peasants and young boys and girls who were put in prison for their Christian faith. These were separated and for them there was a special brainwashing, not only that "communism is good," but "Christianity is dead, Christianity is dead, Christianity is dead. Nobody more believes in Christ, nobody more believes in Christ, you are the only fools."

And so on. And I must tell you that you may know how far this brainwashing went. I do not like to pose here like a hero. I believed that Christianity is dead under this influence. I believed——

Senator DODD. I did not hear that.

Reverend WURMBRAND. I believed that Christianity is dead under this suggestion. Nobody goes more to church. They gave us post cards. I have not seen my wife for 10 years. They gave me post cards, they gave to all of us post cards: "Write to your children and wife; they may come and on that day see you and bring your parcels," so on that day we were shaved; we expected and expected until the evening and nobody came. They had not sent the post cards, but we did not know. Then came the brainwashings. "Your wives are laying in bed with men," obscene words, "Your children hate you. You have nobody to love in the world. You are the only fools. Give up faith. Nobody is more Christians. Christianity is dead."

I believed also that nobody is more a Christian. I had read in the Bible that there will be in the last time the great apostasy, that people will leave the faith and I believed that I lived now this time. But I said to myself if Christianity is dead, I will sit at its tomb and will weep until it arises again, just as Mary Magdalene sat at the tomb of Jesus and wept until Jesus showed himself. Then when I came out of prison I saw Christianity is not dead. The number of practicing Christians in Rumania according to the figures given by the Communists themselves in 20 years of Communist dictatorship has grown 300 percent.

Senator DODD. How do the Communists use religion for their own purposes if they do?

Revererd WURMBRAND. That is a very tragic side. The worse thing in Rumania has not been the persecution of Christians. The persecution has made the Christians to be of steel. The worst thing has been the corruption of religion. They have put as religious leaders their man. A bishop, a pastor, a preacher, just a man like other man and can commit sins. Now if they found a preacher or somebody else in adultery or in some money irregularity or I do not know what sin, they called him and blackmailed him and said, "Now you must become our man. Otherwise we publish what we have found." Or they found others who were weak ones, whom they promised I do not know what. They never keep their promises. And these men, they put at the leadership of religion everywhere.

They have their bishops, their bishop vicar, their professors of theology, their presidents of the Baptists and Pentacostals and so on. I could give names. I know this from firsthand. Because many of these, when we came out of prison, out of remorse confessed to us what they have done. And now they use these men. With us in Rumania religion is a very great thing. You do not find much religious difference in Rumania. By these weak Christians, the Communists used religion for their propaganda. When the Communists came to power in Rumania, they convoked in the building of our parliament a congress of all the cults. There were 4,000 priests; pastors, rabbis of all religions were there. Our Prime Minister

Groza, said the same things which you hear now in the West. This was in 1945 when they came to power with us. "You know Rumanian communism will not be like Russian communism. We are a democratic communism. We will not persecute the church. We are on the side of monarchy. We will never collectivate agriculture. We are something entirely else and you should be on our side and then we will protect religion and we will give salaries to the priests."

And the priests, good men, simply believed him and cheered him. Priests and bishops one after the other stood up and said, "Well, if your communism is otherwise than the Russian communism, if it will be a good communism, we do not object against communism in principle." And one after the other stood up and praised this form of communism. There was only one in that congress who protested and said that communism can never change, that terror is an essential part of communism, because communism is contrary to human nature.

What would you say if I would take the purse out of your pocket? Everyone wishes to have something. A dog wishes to have a bone, and communism is against human nature because it does not allow you to have anything of yours and so communism must use terror. At that congress there was only one who said these things. This one is now before you.

But what has happened? I went to prison, this was one of the charges against me. I met in prison all those who had praised communism, all those who have collaborated with communism, and they were treated just like me. They had been the fools. There was only one difference that I was in prison with a good conscience and they were with a bad conscience. In prison they had remorse. Religion was used for Communist propaganda in our country.

Just to give you one example: To the Orthodox Church of Rumania foreigners come and see the liturgy and see everything so beautiful. The church is open. They do not understand the language, they do not know what is preached. I will give you the text of the sermon. It was a sermon about an epistle of St. Paul where it was written that Christ is our peace, and so the priest explained, "Christ is our peace. Who is against peace? American imperialists. And who is on the side of the peace? We, the Socialist countries."

So you see that Christ identifies himself with socialism and so on. Such sermons they have. They have used the religion for their own purposes in the country. Then they have used the religion for getting political positions in the West. They are not fools to send in the West representatives of the Communist Party. They send bishops with great beards and beards are always very impressive here in the West, and through these beards they influence the West.

Senator Dodd. I have many more questions, but would you show your wounds and scars, if you have some?

Reverend Wurmbrand. I apologize here before the ladies.

Senator Dodd. Take your time. If ever a man was entitled to time, I think you are.

Reverend Wurmbrand. Look here, look here, look here. Look here, look here. And so the whole body.

Senator Dodd. What is the scar behind your ear?

Reverend Wurmbrand. Here they put the knife and said, "Give accusatory statements against your bishops and against the other pastors. Do you give or not?" And they cut. It is true that they did not cut very deeply.

Senator Dodd. These are all knife wounds?

Reverend Wurmbrand. They tortured by all means. They beat until they broke the bones. They used red-hot irons, they used knives, they used everything. And what was the first thing is not that they beat, not what they did, but how they did it. They interrogated you very politely, and if you did not wish to say what they asked they said, "Well, we have the first. On the 15th you will be beaten and tortured at 10 o'clock in the evening."

Imagine what 14 days were after this. We have had prisoners who during this time, which has been given to them, knocked at the door, "I can't bear it. I will say everything," before they have been tortured.

Senator Dodd. I wish you would turn around before you put your shirt on.

Reverend Wurmbrand. And that it may be very clear, it is not that I boast with these marks. I show to you the tortured body of my country, of my fatherland, and of my church, and they appeal to the American Christians and to all freemen of America to think about our tortured body, and we do not ask you to help us. We ask you only one thing. Do not help our oppressors and do not praise them. You cannot be a Christian and praise the inquisitors of Christians. That is what I have to say.

Senator Dodd. All right. You may put on your clothes. That scar on your right breast, do you remember how that was inflicted?

Reverand Wurmbrand. Yes; by knife.

Senator Dodd. By knife?

Reverend Wurmbrand. By knife. I have been in Oslo. I went to a hospital. There were several physicians. I can give their names. I spoke with them about religion. In the beginning they said, "We are atheists," and then they saw my body and I asked them what treatment do I need. They said: "About treatment, do not ask us. Ask only the one in whom we don't believe, but who has kept you alive, because according to our medical books, you are dead. A man who has what you have, with four vertebras broken, cannot live. According to our medical books, you are dead. If you are alive, then the one in whom we don't believe has kept you alive."

Senator Dodd. I think it is important for our purposes to understand this completely. As I take it, they cut you, but they must have been asking you questions.

Reverend Wurmbrand. Surely, surely. I had worked in the representation of the World Council of Churches in Rumania, and after the war this World Council of Churches made a great relief work and I myself had relationship with the Rumanian patriarchs and with the bishops and with the Baptists and with the Pentacostals and Lutherans and so on, and we worked with all these. And now they wish to make with us in Rumania a great show process, a great show trial as they have made in Hungary with Cardinal Mindszenty and so on, and they wished from me accusatory statements against all these with whom I have had connections, and because I did not wish to give these accusatory statements, I and others have been tortured. This has been the usual thing. Nobody enters in the Rumanian secret police without being beaten, without being tortured. I have been not the worst tortured. The proof is that I am alive. So many died. Nearly all our Catholic bishops have been so handled that they have died, and in that time the Russians were in our country, they decided that the Catholic bishops should be killed. One of the members of the Government has been Gromyko, one of the murderers of Christians. Perhaps you will understand why I call his name.

Senator DODD. Yes; I do.

Reverend WURMBRAND. I have seen Catholic priests, heroes, dying not only for Christ and confessing Christ to the end, but dying for the Pope.

I have heard the word of a Catholic priest, I will not tell his name. He was asked, "Do you still believe in the Pope?" and he said, "Since St. Peter there has always been a Pope, and until Christ will come again there will always be a Pope. And the actual Pope, Pius the 12th, has not made peace with you and never will a Pope shake hands with you." He was trampled under the feet and tortured to death. Under our eyes he was killed. At that time a member of the government who killed this Catholic priest has been Gromyko, and the priest died with the hope that never will a Pope shake hands with his murderers.

Senator DODD. You saw and heard this yourself.

Reverend WURMBRAND. Yes, surely; and it is not only one case. I could never finish if I would tell you what I have seen. I must just pour out before you my heart. I speak for a country and I speak for a church. We are very, very sad there about all these compromises. I must tell you I have been in England before I came to the States, and I have spoken with high Christian officials from England. The Archbishop of Canterbury and many canons and so on have been in our country recently, last year. So I asked Christian leaders—I will not tell names—"Why have you sat at banquets with our inquisitors? I am a little pastor, I cannot interrogate you, but I speak for the others who cannot speak for themselves. Why have you sat at banquets with our inquisitors?"

I was answered, "We are Christians and must have friendship and fellowship with everybody, with the Communists, too. Don't you agree?"

I said, "I can't polemicize with you. I have not read the Bible for 14 years. You must know Christianity better than I. Faintly I remember in the Bible it is written that friendship with the world is hatred toward God. But supposing you must have friendship and fellowship with everybody. How is it that you have had friendship and fellowship only with our inquisitors, and with us never?"

Never have these great men of the West been in the houses of Christian martyrs. I have an only son and I love him. I cannot look to him. He looks like a skeleton. He has hungered. He will never be healthy. And so many of our children died. All these great prelates from the West are great men. I am very little in comparison with them. But I always asked myself, "Well, all right, make friendship with the Communists. But only with the Communists?" They never inquired about us.

I asked them, "Why did you go to see the Pope, who is all right, who does not need your visit? When you have been in Rumania why have you not visited the tombs of the Catholic bishops killed in tortures? Why have you not shed there a tear? Why have you not put there a flower? That is what we expected. Why have you not left 10 pounds? Ten pounds would have been the salvation of a Catholic family there. You go to see the Pope. The Pope is all right.

He has to eat and to drink." But I must say we are very sad there about these compromises with communism. We do not understand. I am a man who does not understand politics. I have not read newspapers for 14 years.

It may be right for a state to have peaceful existence with communism. I do not know. That is a question for Johnson and Goldwater to decide. But the church can never have peaceful coexistence with atheism. Everybody would laugh if I would say that health can peacefully exist with the microbe of tuberculosis, that the FBI can coexist peacefully with gangsters, that the church can peacefully exist with drunkenness, but communism and atheism is much worse than drug addiction and drunkenness. You drink a little wine and the next day it passes, but communism poisons youth and our children since 50 years. How can there be peaceful existence with this on the side of churchmen and the church leadership I cannot understand.

I must say I have been very sad. I have read in your periodicals that, I do not know why, church bodies here ask the admission of Red China in the organization of allied nations. It may be right. I do not know politics. I do not know what this organization of allied nations is, but I ask myself, "You, a church periodical, why don't you write about the tortures inflicted to Chinese Christians by the Communists? That is your business and leave the business of politics to the Senate and like this."

I express here the grief and the great pain of a suffering country and of a suffering church, and I apologize if I am a little unpolite.

Senator Dodd. You were the representative of the World Council of Christian Churches?

Reverend Wurmbrand. I was one of the workers of the office of the World Council of Churches. This man who gives me a certificate, this Pastor Hedenquist, was at that time one of the leaders of the Council of Churches who came to Rumania.

Mr. Sourwine. You were responding to the chairman's question about what had been asked of you under interrogation. Did you complete that answer?

Reverend Wurmbrand. Well, it is a very interesting thing. Jesus says that the children of this world are wiser than the children of light. You are a political body. You interrogate me about what I have been asked about the World Council of Churches. The World Council of Churches never put to me this question.

Senator Dodd. Never what?

Reverend Wurmbrand. They have never put to me the question, "You have been arrested. One of the main subjects of your interrogation was that you represented us in Rumania. Please tell us what have you been interrogated about?"

I was never asked by them. The secret police wished to know everybody with whom they worked and with whom we had connections and so on. One of the great purposes of their interrogation was to know how they could win the World Council of Churches for their position.

Mr. Sourwine. How they could win?

Reverend Wurmbrand. The Council of Churches to defend their position.

Mr. Sourwine. How did you answer that one?

Reverend WURMBRAND. Well, I hoped—I must say that I was mistaken in the answers which I gave—I hoped that the World Council of Churches will never be won to their position.

Senator DODD. Will never be what?

Reverend WURMBRAND. Won for their position.

Senator DODD. Work for their position?

Reverend WURMBRAND. That they will never, so I had hoped. And now when I came out I read last month there was a sitting of the World Council of Churches in Geneva, in which they took the following decision, a very nice decision: "We ask America to stop its fight against communism, and we ask also the Communist governments to stop their fight to overthrow the social regime everywhere," which was a very nice decision. "We ask both parts to keep peace."

But in the East nobody published this decision of theirs. Nobody in the East has the slightest idea of this decision. So this disarms only the West. Such decisions are taken. They look very fine. The purpose has been accomplished.

Mr. SOURWINE. In effect, the sole accomplishment has been to ask the West to stop its fight?

Reverend WURMBRAND. Yes.

Mr. SOURWINE. You mentioned questions about the World Council of Churches. Was there more than one, or was there just the single question of how they could win it for their purposes?

Reverend WURMBRAND. No; there were also other questions; what relief they sent and to whom they gave this relief and what was the political purpose of this relief, and so on. They considered then the World Council of Churches—that was in 1948—they considered the World Council of Churches as an American spy organization. They do not consider it any more like that.

Mr. SOURWINE. You were being questioned by the Rumanian secret police, were you not?

Reverend WURMBRAND. Yes.

Mr. SOURWINE. When you say they wanted to know how they could win the World Council of Churches for their purposes, did you mean for the purposes of Rumania?

Reverend WURMBRAND. No, no, no; for the purposes of communism, for the purposes of the whole Communist world.

Mr. SOURWINE. In other words, the Rumanian secret police are, in your opinion at least, just like any other Communist secret police?

Reverend WURMBRAND. Sure, there is no difference at all, and our interrogations, if they were important ones as mine, they went to Moscow. I know it from the Orthodox priest, Vasile Leon, who has been kidnaped from Austria and he has been brought to Moscow. In Moscow he has been interrogated about me. In Moscow they knew everything about Rumania. They worked hand in hand. At that time the secret Rumanian police had Soviet advisers.

Mr. SOURWINE. I think you have touched on this, but can you perhaps give us a little more on the subject? What has been the policy and practice of the Communists with respect to religion in countries where they have come into power?

Reverend WURMBRAND. They used three great instruments. First of all, the persecution, to make everybody afraid. They never accepted that they have put anybody in prison for religious motives. They found always political motives. Now I will give you the political motives.

A Unitarian pastor, a friend of mine, has been put in prison and sentenced to 7 years under the charge that on a Christmas Eve he has said that Jesus being a baby Herod wished to kill him but his holy mother fled with him to Egypt. That was the charge. "Aha, you meant us under Herod, and you hope Nasser will be on the side of the imperialists and therefore you mentioned Egypt."

Another friend of mine, a pastor, was sentenced to 15 years in prison. He was one of the greatest saints whom I have ever seen in life. The charge against him was he preached on a Sunday morning in a village about John 21 where it is said that the Lord walked on the seashore and he saw the apostles and asked them, "Have you something to eat?" They said, "We have not," and then Jesus said, "Throw your nets on the right side."

So the pastor preached from the pulpit. He asked, "Have you something to eat?" and when he asked, "Have you something to eat?" everybody began to weep, because with us, peasants have nothing to eat. After the collectivization of agriculture our peasants have nothing to eat. Peasant children do not see milk and fruit. Everything goes to the collective and from the collective perhaps to Vietnam. Nobody knows where it goes. Our population does not see. They began to weep because they had nothing to eat and then the pastor, not knowing in what world he is, said, "Dear children, you have nothing to eat because you throw your nets on the left side. You must throw them on the right side." He meant the side of the clemency and of the goodness of God.

The next day there was the secret police, "Aha, you have said not to go to the leftwing with the Communists but with the right side, the imperialists."

The man got 15 years of prison.

So there has been, first of all, this method of persecution. There has been, secondly, the method of corruption. We live in the times of the abomination of the desolation of the holy places. There have always been bad Popes and good Popes and bad priests and good priests. For the first time in church history the leadership of churches is dominated by the central committee of an avowed atheistic power. The central committee of the party decides who must be patriarch, who must be Baptist preacher, Pentacostal preacher, and so on. Everywhere they have found weak men or men with some sin. Those they have put in the leadership of churches and so you could hear in our theological seminary in Bucharest the theology that God has given three revelations—once through Moses, second through Jesus, the third through Karl Marx, and so on.

Religion is corrupted from within. Religion has been widely used and is still as the tools of Communist politics. The priests everywhere had to propagate the collectivization of agriculture and everywhere when Communists have something important to do, knowing the influence of religion, priests and pastors are put to preach these things.

Mr. Sourwine. Have the Communists shown themselves to be opposed only to Christianity, or to all religions?

Reverend Wurmbrand. To all the religions. The Jewish religion has been persecuted just as the Christian religion. In the prison of Gherla we had a whole room with rabbis who were in prisons. We had in prison the Moslem priests and so on.

Mr. Sourwine. Did they segregate the rabbis in one room——

Reverend WURMBRAND. Yes.

Mr. SOURWINE. The Christians in another, and——

Reverend WURMBRAND. No, no, they were at a time kept with us, but the rabbis, because they had to respect certain dietary laws and the Sabbath and so on, they separated them in order not to provoke collision with other prisoners.

Mr. SOURWINE. Did the prison authorities permit the Jews to follow their dietary requirements?

Reverand WURMBRAND. Yes.

Mr. SOURWINE. To practice their religion?

Reverend WURMBRAND. Yes; under one form. They could follow the dietary rules, not eating everything which has been given to them. That is all. They did not give them any special food.

Senator DODD. They did not give them any special diet?

Reverend WURMBRAND. No; no special diet for Jews. Neither do the Moslems eat pork and so they did not get anything special.

Senator DODD. Were the rabbis subjected to the same kind of torture that you suffered?

Reverend WURMBRAND. Yes; sure, sure. There was no difference in this. I must say it may look anecdotic for you. I had a discussion once with the commandant of the prison of Targulacna, and he said, "We are not like the Fascists who made the racial differences and persecuted the Jews and Hungarians. We are not so. Look around you. We keep in prison Rumanians, Hungarians, and Jews all alike. We don't make racial differences."

Mr. SOURWINE. That could be interpreted to mean that he was saying people of the Jewish faith were being persecuted for their religious activity, but not for their race.

Is it true that there is no anti-Semitism in Rumania?

Reverend WURMBRAND. There is anti-Semitism. Just before we left the country, everywhere where Jews were in high positions as chief engineers or directors in ministry and so on, they were silenced and put to lower functions.

Mr. SOURWINE. Would you expand on that?

Senator DODD. Just repeat it.

Reverend WURMBRAND. Yes, yes. Just before we left Rumania, a few weeks before we left Rumania, all kinds of Jews who were chief engineers or directors or something great in different institutions have been put to lower positions just because they were Jews.

Senator DODD. To lower positions?

Reverend WURMBRAND. To lower positions.

Mr. SOURWINE. Not because of religion?

Reverend WURMBRAND. No, no.

Mr. SOURWINE. Just as a matter of racial prejudice?

Reverend WURMBRAND. Sure. They could have been atheists. They were even members of the Communist Party, but if they were of Jewish origin, they were put to lower positions. From the secret police all the Jews have been driven out.

Mr. SOURWINE. Are there any Buddhists in Rumania?

Reverend WURMBRAND. Buddhists? No; we have none. Perhaps a few intellectuals, just a few.

Mr. SOURWINE. Have the Communists done anything, to your knowledge, to try to win position and influence for Communist agents in the religious community of the free world?

Reverend WURMBRAND. Sure. We had a professor, Justin Moisescu.

Mr. SOURWINE. Moisescu?

Reverend WURMBRAND. Moisescu, yes. He was a professor. He had never been a priest. Truly a very clever and a very cultured man. He was professor of church history, but a layman. With us there has been a law that you can't be professor in a theological institute unless you are a priest. So he resigned. He didn't wish to be a priest.

And then, what discussions he had with the secret police he knows, he was known in the whole country as a whoremonger, as a drunkard, nobody appreciated him. At once we heard that in a few weeks he had become priest, bishop, metropolitan of Yasi. That is the highest function with us after the patriarch.

Mr. SOURWINE. That is the Rumanian Orthodox Church?

Reverend WURMBRAND. In the Rumanian Orthodox Church. Whatever will be the consequences for me, I have told you how I have been threatened, and these threatenings are not simple words.

Recently from Italy two Rumanians have been kidnaped. We have their names. And I know what can happen to me. But I will tell you this Justin Moisescu personally has denounced a group of 400 Christian peasants from his own bishopric. I have been imprisoned with them. He has denounced the priests whom he ordained when he knew that they said some counterrevolutionary word.

He has a very impressive beard and he has come out to the free world and was accepted as a bishop, and those in the West believe that they speak with the Orthodox Church of Rumania and they speak with the secret police of Rumania. And now the interesting thing is I would not mind accepting men like him and like Gromatca, this arch traitor and others. I don't mind that they are accepted in the West. But I ask myself in every bargain, in every business, both parts must win. I give you the product but you must give me the dollars for it. We accept your traitors. What does the East accept from us? If we had posed to Rumania this question, "We will accept Justin Moisescu, you must accept a Bible society in Rumania," we would have it. But we accept without asking for it. Justin Moisescu is a member of the secret police. They sent to America the priest Liviu Stan. Everybody knows Liviu Stan is a man of the Communists. When the Communists came to power he was among the first ones who put posters on our walls that Christians must vote and go with the Communists. These posters were signed and the others by this Liviu Stan. The Communists in Rumania are not so stupid to send here a man who will say, "I come from the side of the Communist Party." Liviu Stan came as a representative of the Orthodox Church of Rumania. And so they have many men. They have sent recently a priest, Ananaia.

Now that is a very interesting thing about this priest, Ananaia. This priest, Ananaia, has been with me in prison. He has been 10 years in prison. He has been beaten. He has passed through brainwashing. And they have such a confidence in brainwashing that they had the confidence to send him to the West and he does their work.

Senator DODD. He is a priest in good standing, and of what church?

Reverend WURMBRAND. In the Orthodox church.

I speak out of the pain of a heart. I can't polemicize. I am a very little pastor. I can't polemicize with great religious bodies, but

I am a man who has read nothing for 14 years. And now I came out to the West. I had always been very interested in missions and I wished to know what happens in missions. I took in hand the International Review of Missions, edited by the World Council of Churches, and I read there in the issue of January that in Rumania, orthodoxism and protestantism grow in an atmosphere of full religious liberty.

If the man who wrote this has not taken thousands of dollars from the Rumanian secret police, he deserves to be hanged for stupidity. He could have taken money for this. I believe he has not taken money. And then I wrote to them a letter, and said, "Either you lie or I lie. If I lie, I promise that never more will I be a pastor. If you lie you have to withdraw. Now to see if I lie or you lie I ask you to answer the following 20 questions, if you say there is full religious liberty in Rumania.

"Where is the office of the World Council of Churches of Religion in Rumania? It has offices everywhere. In the Communist countries it has none.

"Where is the Bible Society? We have no Bible Society. Show me one Bible printed in 20 years. We have no such thing. Tell me the name of one Christian who for 20 years could publish a book. Give me the name of one Christian professor of humanistic sciences in our country. Tell me one Sunday school in Bucharest where it can be attended.

"Tell me where is the YMCA in Rumania. Where are the pastors Ghelbegeanu, Vacareanu, and so on? They are in prison.

"Please answer to me these questions. If you have received answers, I have received answers."

There is no possible answers. It is not right for Christians to mock our sufferings. The Communists have mocked us enough. Don't praise our inquisitors. That is the only thing which we ask.

I apologize before these great Christians bodies. I am really a very little man but I speak for the great saints who suffer in prison. It is not right to praise our inquisitors or to think that now they have become better.

Mr. Sourwine. Are the restrictive measures imposed upon the exercise of religion in Rumania today as stringent as they were 10 or 15 years ago?

Reverend Wurmbrand. No; they are no more stringent and I will explain to you why. I have been in a very poor family, a family with five children. Generally our men are very poor with us, unbelievably poor.

My salary when I left Rumania was $28. You say it is little, $28 a week. It was $28 a month. My son was not allowed to finish his studies because of my condemnation. He worked as a building worker and had $30 a month. Our bishop has $70 a month. And now our population is very, very poor.

Senator Dodd. When you say dollars, you mean the equivalent?

Reverend Wurmbrand. Yes; the equivalent of $70. Now I was in a very poor familiy with five little children, and I caressed a child and the mother said to me, "This child is so good, it doesn't weep even when it is hungry." It had given up weeping because the child knew it is useless to weep. You can't get food. And so this child was not beaten, because it didn't weep any more. The Rumanian people does not weep any more. And, therefore, it must not be beaten any more.

The Rumanian people, as well as the other peoples behind the Iron Curtain, are desperate. They have abandoned hope that they will ever be released. For years we have heard a broadcast station: "Rebel against communism, rebel against communism," and when we rebelled we were abandoned.

And we see how our oppressors are helped. I will tell you a scene. Believe me, God is here. I tell you the scene just as it happened. It was in the years of brainwashing, the 14th year of prison. We are gathered to a meeting, and Major Alexandrescu, the commandant of the prison of Gherla, delivered us a speech and said:

You fools, you set for 15 or 20 years in prison and expected the Americans to come. You expected the Americans will come and release you. Now I will give you the news. The Americans come but not to release you. They come to help us, to help us, to make business with us, to make trade with us. You fools have not known. The Americans if you beg them, they give you nothing. If you insult them, if you mock them, they give you money. We have been more clever than you.

These are words which I have heard myself. Such things have happened in our country.

Mr. SOURWINE. Are there any open churches in Rumania today, which anyone may attend?

Reverend WURMBRAND. Just I didn't finish this question. So there is a relaxation in what sense? Our people has given up the fight. Political underground movements don't exist any more with us. They have no such. And so everything has quieted down in the country, and so they don't need any more of the same terror. I have been for years in prison with thieves and murderers. Even before having been put in prison I have been chaplain of a prison. A thief after he has stolen is a gentleman. He gives to the waiters the greatest tips and he invites girls and he invites you and he orders the best wines. He has not worked for his money. And such thieves are the Communists. They have stolen half of Europe, they have stolen Russia, too. They have stolen a great part of Asia. And now they have what they have stolen and they are gentlemen and they expect the next occasion to steal again.

In this sense there is a relaxation with us, but it is not an essential one. We continue to have the avowed dictatorship of an atheistic party. We have one party. There can be no religious freedom where there is one party. We have elections. Now a joke is made with us that when God created Adam, He created only one woman, Eve, and He said to Adam, "You are free to choose for wife whomsoever you wish." But there was only Eve. And so are the elections with us.

Our Government doesn't mind old women coming to church, but our childhood, our youth is poisoned with atheism. We are not allowed to counteract, and what bitter fruits will come out of this seed nobody can know.

Now you have asked another question, do we have open churches in Rumania? If somebody comes to Rumania—it is another situation in Russia—if somebody comes to Rumania, he is really impressed.

The Orthodox liturgy is something very beautiful. It is grand. And if you come in Rumania you see thousands of churches open, liturgies, sermons, many people in the church. And I have spoken with Americans who have been there and have told me, "I was very impressed." And now there is really a certain religious liberty. In Rumania you are allowed to say as much as you like that God is good. You are not allowed to say that the Devil is bad. St. John the Baptist could have saved his life if he had said: "Repent because the kingdom of heaven is near." Nobody would have touched him. He was touched when he said, "You, Herod, are bad."

If Christ would have delivered a thousand "Sermons on the Mount" they would not have crucified Him. They crucified Him when He said, "You vipers," then He was crucified.

In Rumania you can say God is good but you can't say "communism is cruel, they commit atrocities, it is a crime to poison children with atheism." If you do this you go to prison. There are many priests, rabbis, and pastors who compromise and don't put the dot on the "i." There exists the real church and the real religion and that which compromises.

Mr. SOURWINE. Are there churchmen in Rumania today who willingly cooperate with the Communist authorities?

Reverend WURMBRAND. Surely. The Orthodox hierarchy nearly entirely. Of the Catholic hierarchy, not one. The Catholic bishops died in prison, all except four. These four have house arrest. At the Vatican council no Catholic bishop was allowed to come. Came a Catholic priest, a well-known traitor, Augustine, who is the real leader of the Catholic Church; the leadership of the Baptists, for example, is entirely in the hands of the Communists.

I have here a document which I present to the Senate, a list of 150 Russian Baptist pastors recently deported to Siberia. Not all arrived in Siberia. Many died of tortures.

Senator DODD. Can you talk a little more slowly? I could get your pronunciation better.

Reverend WURMBRAND. This is a list of 150 Baptist pastors of Russia who have been recently deported to Siberia. I have the names, the addresses, the names of their wives, of their children. They have not all arrived to Siberia, because of the tortures many died.

Senator DODD. These were Rumanians?

Reverend WURMBRAND. No, no, Russians. And I give it to the Senate.

Mr. SOURWINE. Mr. Chairman, do you wish this list and the document of transmittal to go into the record? There is an English translation to be made.

Senator DODD. Yes; I believe it should be in the record.

Mr. SOURWINE. Will you hand that list to the reporter?

(The list and the document appear in the appendix of this volume.)

Senator DODD. I don't quite understand this. These are 400 Russian Baptists?

Reverend WURMBRAND. 150.

Senator DODD. Were they in Rumania?

Reverend WURMBRAND. No, no, they are Russians. We got it from Russia. Here I have another very interesting document.

Mr. SOURWINE. If you would excuse me, please, I believe the Senator's question raises a point you should clear up. How do you have this information about Russia? Have you been in Russia?

Reverend WURMBRAND. I have worked for years secret missionary work among the Russian soldiers who occupied our country. I speak Russian fluently, and we brought many Russian soldiers to Christ. To preach Christ to the Russians means Heaven on earth. They seek the Gospel as the thirsty soil seeks water. They have not known Him. The beauty of the Gospel you know it when you preach it to Russians; how they live it and how they enjoy it, and so I have made some connections.

In a public sitting I can't say how I have arrived to have these lists.

Mr. SOURWINE. You know it to be authentic?

Reverend WURMBRAND. Personally I can tell you from where I have this list, but it is absolutely authentic. It can be controlled. Surely in a public sitting I can't say how I have received it.

I present to the Senate also a very interesting document, the most interesting I have ever known in this matter, the document, "Li Wei Han." It is a letter of the Central Committee of the Communist Party of China addressed to the Central Committee of the Communist Party of Cuba. Now recently they have quarreled but this letter is an older one in which they teach how to win the leadership of the churches for communism, how to make that the Communists should be leaders of the churches. It is an unequaled document of Machiavelianism.

We have lived these things but never have I seen it put on paper as this.

Mr. SOURWINE. May I suggest this be printed as an appendix to the record, Mr. Chairman?

Senator DODD. Yes.

(The letter referred to will be found in the appendix.)

Senator DODD. I take it what you have been telling us must be more or less common knowledge in Rumania, is it?

Reverend WURMBRAND. Yes; surely.

Senator DODD. Would it be accurate to deduce that the embassy officials of the several countries must have heard it too?

Reverend WURMBRAND. Yes, surely. Everybody knows, but there are many here in the West who don't wish to know.

Senator DODD. Why not?

Reverend WURMBRAND. They don't wish to be troubled in their quietness. They close their eyes before this menace. I have met men who simply close their eyes when I told them about these things. They know that they are true. But they have a certain policy of friendly relationship with the Communist countries, and they are very honest men, but they are duped exactly as we were duped in Rumania.

Wherever the Communists came in the beginning, they said the same thing which I read here in newspapers and in periodicals. "You know Stalin's communism has been very bad, but Yugoslavian communism or another kind of communism, this is very good."

A little lion in its first days you can play with him just like with a puppy. When he becomes great, only then he is a lion. Yugoslavian communism is this little communism. And American communism is a very little one and English communism is a very little one. When they grow, when they can do whatever they will to do, then only we can see them. With us, in the beginning, we also had a very nice communism. I have seen in Rumanian Communist demonstrations signs with the slogan, "God Save the King." I have seen the Communist Secretaries of State making great crosses, showing themselves as being on the side of religion and making compliments to religion and bowing to religion and saying they are Democrats. In the beginning, they have put in prison party members who said that the agriculture must be collectivized. And they have gone together with the bourgeois party, with the Liberal Party of Tatorescu and with other Democrats.

I have seen in the West Social Democrats collaborate with them. In Rumania, I have seen dying Social Democrats in the same cell with me; they died. Communists in Rumania, too, were nice until they had the whole power in hand. When they had the whole power in hand, they have done things exactly as in Russia, and so they will do everywhere. There is no difference.

Mr. SOURWINE. You mentioned demonstrations by the Communists. Does Rumania have anything like the demonstrations that are so prevalent in this country, demonstrations against the Government's activities or against its policies?

Reverend WURMBRAND. Nobody can say a word of criticism. Such a thing doesn't even enter in the mind of somebody. I will tell you something which may be laughable for you. It is very tragical with us. But the story is just as I tell you. I know the man. A man was in a barbershop in a little town, Sibiu. While the barber shaved him, he said to the barber: "What should I do? My hair falls." The barber said, "Very well, I will make you a friction but you must not be anxious about this. The most intelligent people of the world have been bald." On the other seat there was an officer of the secret police and he said to the barber, "What have you said now?"

"I have said that the most intelligent people of the world are bald."

"So, you assert that Stalin has not been intelligent." It is a question of laughter for you but it is tragical with us. Nobody dares to say a word.

I stopped in Newark, and in Philadelphia, a demonstration against the war in Vietnam. I had not this clerical suit on. I stopped the demonstrators and I undressed myself to the belt. Afterwards I heard that it is illegal here in the States, and that I could have gone to prison for this. I undressed myself.

Senator DODD. It would have been all right on the bathing beach.

Reverend WURMBRAND. Yes; it was not on the beach. And I told them, "This have Communists done to me. Do you think that American Christians should fight against communism?" So they surrounded me and asked me, "Why have Communists done to you this?" I said to them, "Suppose that I am a murderer. Do you agree that a murderer should be tortured? Has Oswald been tortured? Has Ruby been tortured with you?" They all said, "No; murderers have not been tortured." I continued: "Then know that I have not be charged with murder. I am a clergyman." They stopped the demonstration. In Philadelphia there was again such a demonstration. I am not a man of politics. I can't speak for the war of Vietnam or against the war in Vietnam. I speak this general principle that Christians must be on the side of righteousness. They must never be on the side of the inquisitors of Christians. They must be on the side of the victims of the inquisitors, they must be on the side of the Christians.

In Philadelphia there was a great meeting. A pastor with clerical suit, a Presbyterian pastor, delivered a speech in which he praised Communists and said that Communists are all right and it is stupid to fight against them. I have learned something from the Communists. In a minute—after—the pastor was no more in the pulpit, I was in the pulpit. I said: "Now I will speak about communism. What do you know about communism? And I will show you my credentials, how I have studied communism." I undressed myself to the belt. I did not know that all these bad reporters are there and took pictures. And I showed them my body. "That is what Communists do to Christians, and you, Pastor, why don't you make demonstrations, if you are a Christian and if you have youth in you and vigor, why don't you demonstrate before the Soviet and Rumanian Embassies and the other embassies against torturing Christians?" And then the public, which has been there booed him and shouted to him "Judas."

These are Judases. They may be all right innerly, I don't know their hearts, but I think that Christians, if they wish to demonstrate, they should demonstrate against those who have recently deported 150 Baptist pastors.

Mr. SOURWINE. The subcommittee has received substantial information to the effect that the Rumanian Communist Government has infiltrated into this country Communist-trained clergy with other missions than those of a spiritual nature. Do you have any information about that?

Reverend WURMBRAND. Rumanian Communists are very interested in the fact that you have here, in the States, something like 300,000 Americans of Rumanian origin who speak the Rumanian language and are Orthodox.

The Rumanians have a bishop, Bishop Viorel Trifa, who is anti-Communist and the Communists wish to win these 300,000 on their side. They can't very well win them for communism, but they can win them for a leftwing Christianity which supports communism. They have sent here several men, Moisescu, Liviu Stan, and so on. These don't come with Communist slogans but with the words: "You must love your Rumanian fatherland. * * * You must have connections with the Rumanian patriarchy." When I came out from Rumania I saw for the first time a Rumanian newspaper which appears in Bucharest, and which nobody in Bucharest has ever seen. The Voice of the Fatherland it is called, and in the fatherland nobody sees this newspaper. Only your American Rumanians see it and in France. I have never seen it. My son looked at it, and we have never seen it. In this newspaper you read about priests and churches. In our newspapers you will never have a word about the church. There you have pictures of priests and monasteries and how fine it is and so on. They make this propaganda, surely.

Senator DODD. You mean this paper is only distributed in the free world?

Reverend WURMBRAND. Only in the free world. They have at midnight, which corresponds to I don't know what hour here in the United States, it is noon or I don't know what, they have religious services which are jammed in Rumania, but they are emitted from Rumania. We have no religious services on the broadcasts. These are broadcast religious services only that the Americans should know how fine the Communists are and that they have religious services.

Mr. SOURWINE. Are you saying that the religious services of the Rumanian Orthodox Church——

Reverend WURMBRAND. Yes.

Mr. SOURWINE (continuing). Are broadcast in Rumania at a time which is midnight in Rumania?

Reverend WURMBRAND. Yes.

Mr. SOURWINE. Beamed to the Western World?

REVEREND WURMBRAND. Yes; sure.

Mr. SOURWINE. To the free world?

Reverend WURMBRAND. Sure.

Mr. SOURWINE. And not broadcast in Rumania?

Reverend WURMBRAND. Sure. In Rumania, nobody hears them.

Mr. SOURWINE. Of course, a broadcast beamed from Rumania to the United States necessarily will have enough power to be picked up in Rumania if anyone wanted to tune in.

Reverend WURMBRAND. First of all, it is a very inconvenient hour. It is midnight for us. Secondly, in Rumania it is jammed.

Mr. SOURWINE. It is what?

Reverend WURMBRAND. Jammed.

Mr. SOURWINE. They jam it in Rumania?

Reverend WURMBRAND. They jam it in Rumania.

Mr. SOURWINE. So that even those who know about it, who might try to pick it up——

Reverend WURMBRAND. It is jammed. You can't hear it in Rumania.

Mr. SOURWINE. Suppose a group of persons were called together trying to tune in that broadcast above the jamming. Would there be reprisals against them? Is it an illegal thing?

Reverend WURMBRAND. In this moment, no reprisals would be taken. No reprisals are taken today if somebody hears foreign broadcasts. But everything is noted. What happens with us? We have waves of terror. We have had a great wave of terror from 1948 and 1949 which lasted until 1955. We had the relax until 1958 when nobody was arrested but everything was noted.

Then in 1959 came again a wave of terror, and all those who were noted for years before were taken in. And now the whole spy work continues with us. You are not arrested. But everybody knows that he is spied out and that everything is noted. How far this inner spy net goes is unimagined. In a little townlet of ours there is a little Baptist church with only 22 members. The pastor of that church told me that he is the informer of the secret police and that he knows three members of his church who give information against him. So it was in the church in which I was. The servant of the church had the order to inform who comes to me. I had no salary. So, usually men who came to me brought a little parcel with food and clothes and so on. The servant had to spy out who comes with parcels. In the smallest churches you have five or six who have to spy out what the others do. One neighbor spies the other. Children spy on their father and so on. It is without end so nobody dares to do a thing.

Senator DODD. I am somewhat interested in these interrogations to which you were subjected. If I understand you correctly, they lasted for hours; is that right?

Reverend WURMBRAND. Yes; surely.

Senator DODD. Without going into a lengthy explanation, what did they ask you?

Reverend WURMBRAND. Well, they asked many things. First of all they wished to know who has said counterrevolutionary things of all the bishops and priests and pastors and laymen whom I knew. Who has spoken against the Government. Who has something against the Government. How we organized and so on, without end. And now at a certain moment I was tired with being beaten. They told me at a certain moment, "Mr. Wurmbrand, supposing that you are not a counterrevolutionary, you are a well-known pastor in the whole country and everybody had confidence in you and you spoke with bishops and all kinds of men and you have been in so many villages and towns and everybody confessed to you and so forth. Tell us who are the counterrevolutionaries. Don't speak about your activity. You are all right. You are not a counterrevolutionary. But then show your loyalty toward our Government, tell us who the counterrevolutionaries are. Are you disposed to do so?" So, I said, "Yes; I am disposed."

When they heard that I am disposed, they asked me: "Do you smoke, do you wish liquors?" Everything I could have at that moment. And he knew, the officer, that he will receive another star there if he gets from me this information. And then he asked me now, "Who are the counterrevolutionaries?" I said, "As you know I have worked on an international scale, so I can tell you the counterrevolutionaries not only in Rumania but even in Russia."

Oh, he was so glad. I said: "In Russia, you have had as Secretary of State for Internal Affairs, Yagoda. Yagoda has killed thousands of people as counterrevolutionaries. Then you have discovered who has been the counterrevolutionary: Yagoda has been. Yagoda has been shot as counterrevolutionary.

"Then you have had as Secretary of State for Internal Affairs, Beria, and Beria has killed other thousands of people as counterrevolutionaries. Then you have found out who has been the counterrevolutionary: Beria. Why do you seek the counterrevolutionaries in the church? Seek them in your own party. And in Rumania it has been the same thing."

Communists are not only anti-Christian. They are anti everything. They are anti their own comrades.

I have been in prison. I have been there with Lucretiu Patrascanu, the great Communist leader, who has brought communism to power in our country. He was put in prison and tortured until be became mad.

My wife has been in prison with Gheorghe Cristescu. Everybody in Rumania knows the founder of communism in Rumania, who has been in prison for communism under the bourgeois. He has been with my wife together, and he said to my wife, "Forty years ago I fought for the 8-hour labor day and now my Communist Party has come to power and I have to work 14 hours a day."

They are anti absolutely everything. It is not only anti-Christian.

Senator DODD. What was the name of the prominent woman Communist in Rumania?

Reverend WURMBRAND. Ana Pauker, and she was also in prison.

Senator DODD. Do you know her?

Reverend WURMBRAND. Yes, yes, surely; she has also been in prison, and she has been kept a short time and then afterward she died of cancer.

Mr. SOURWINE. I have no more questions, sir.

Senator DODD. We don't have any more questions. Do you have anything more you want to say, Pastor?

Reverend WURMBRAND. I want to say something. I owe it to those with whom I have been in prison. I have told you so many sad things. I don't wish to end with this note. I must tell you that in these great tortures and this great suffering, Christians have shown themselves as saints and as heroes, and if I am allowed to conclude with just one scene which I have seen myself.

It was at the canal. With us, 150,000 men and women have been arrested to build a canal. Beaten, tortured, hungry, without anything, they had to build a canal.

Senator DODD. Build a canal?

Reverend WURMBRAND. Yes; a canal, the Danube Canal. My wife has worked and shoveled the earth. At this canal, there was a religious brigade of 400 men, bishops, priests, peasants who loved Christ, sectarians and so on, all who were for religious motives in prison.

Over this brigade criminals have been put, and to the criminals it has been promised that they will be released if they torture these Christians. This promise has never been kept. But imagine a criminal who is sentenced for life, if he knows that he has such a hope. If they saw you in this brigade making a cross as it is a habit with us in Rumania, or folding your hands or saying a word about God you were beaten to death.

And now a Sunday morning the political officer of the prison comes, the whole brigade is gathered, and just at random he sees a young man. He calls him, "What is your name?" He says the name. "What are you by profession?" He said, "A priest." And then mocking the Communist said, "Do you still believe in God?"

This priest knew that if he says yes, this is the last day of his life. We all looked to him. For a few seconds he was silent. Then his face began to shine and then he opened his mouth and with a very humble but with a very decided voice he said: "Mr. Lieutenant, when I became a priest I knew that during church history thousands of Christians and priests have been killed for their faith, and notwithstanding I became a Christian and I became a priest. I knew what I became. And as often as I entered the altar clad in this beautiful ornate which priests wear I promised to God, "If I will wear the uniform of a prisoner, then also I will serve Him. Mr. Lieutenant, prison is not an argument against religion. I love Christ from all my heart."

I am sad that I can't give the intonation with which he said these words. I think that Juliet when she spoke about Romeo, she spoke like that. We were ashamed because we—we believed in Christ. This man loved Christ as a bride loves the bridegroom. This man has been beaten and tortured to death. But this is Rumania. Rumania is a country which is mocked, which is oppressed, but deep in the hearts of the people is a great esteem and a great praise for those who have suffered. The love to God, the love to Christ, the love to fatherland has never ceased. My country will live. With this I finish.

Senator Dodd. Your testimony has certainly been very impressing.

(At this point, a member of the audience later identified as L. D. O'Flaherty, addressed the Chair).

Mr. O'Flaherty. Mr. Chairman, we have pretty substantial reason to believe that our brother is in danger of his life, and I don't know what steps we could take to have him claim asylum here. He has asylum in France, but we fear for his life because as he has told you, they have told him they will bump him off, get a gangster to bump him off. What arrangements if any—I am not a politician or a political science scholar—what arrangements could be made for his asylum in this country? Can he make a declaration to secure asylum here for his protection?

We know individuals have followed him from city to city unknown to him, and I ask this openly here.

Senator Dodd. Would you identify yourself? I didn't get your name.

Mr. O'Flaherty. O'Flaherty. L. D. O'Flaherty.

Senator Dodd. O'Flaherty?

Mr. O'Flaherty. I am a businessman, a Christian businessman. I am a director in a certain organization here that is giving him support, Friends of Israel. On that basis I make this request. I don't think he understands the danger.

Reverend Wurmbrand. We have a God who protects us. We have the angels around us.

Senator Dodd. I think we had better discuss this matter privately with the pastor after the public hearing. I don't think it is a matter which should be discussed publicly.

Mr. O'Flaherty. Thank you.

Senator Dodd. We will adjourn this hearing now subject to further call.

(Whereupon, at 11:50 a.m., the subcommittee adjourned subject to the call of the Chair.)

APPENDIX

Translation (French)

[Translator's Note: Since this material is a re-re-translation, a literal translation from the French is given below—so as not to lose any more of the flavor of the original text (Chinese).—EH.]

"LI WEI HAN" DOCUMENT

> Important documents are lost in the succession of daily events. "DIFFUSION—INFORMATION DOCUMENTAIRE" makes a point of furnishing texts in the form of pamphlets, presenting one document at a time.

Full translation of a document published in 1959 by: "The Foreign Language Press [Publications] of Peking for the use of the Latin American section of the Liaison Department of the Chinese Communist Party".

This document defines, in its own words, the [various] development stages of the "dialectical struggle within religion for the purpose of progressively replacing the religious element therein by the Marxist element, * * * and of leading the Catholics to destroy, by themselves and on their own account, the divine images which they themselves had created."

PUBLISHED BY THE FOREIGN LANGUAGE PRESS OF PEKING FOR THE EXCLUSIVE USE OF THE LATIN AMERICAN SECTION OF THE LIAISON DEPARTMENT OF THE CHINESE COMMUNIST PARTY

Printed in the People's Republic of China

THE CATHOLIC CHURCH AND CUBA

(Action Program)

The Catholic Church, which has its headquarters in Rome, is a reactionary organization which stirs up counter-revolutionary activities within the People's democracies. So that the People's Democracies may continue to advance via Socialism and Communism, it is necessary, first of all, to do away with the influence of the Catholic Church and with the activities which it carries on. The Catholic Church is neither sterile nor impotent; on the contrary, its power must be recognized and a number of measures must be taken to block its way.

When the political struggle and the production forces have attained a high level of production [rate of productivity] it will be possible to destroy it [the Church]. That is the objective to be attained and that is what we are fighting for. To make a frontal attack and to strike [it] in the face, as we will be poorly equipped and as we will not have educated the masses properly, would result only in giving the Church an even greater control over the masses because they would then feel in sympathy with it and clandestinely support its counter-revolutionary activities. It must also be prevented that the counter-revolutionary leaders of the Church would appear as martyrs. The line of action to be followed against the Church consists in instructing, educating, persuading, convincing, and gradually awakening and fully developing the political consciousness of the Catholics through obtaining their participation in study groups and political activities. We must undertake [engage in] the dialectical struggle within religion through the instrumentality of "activists" (militant Communists).[1] We will progressively replace the religious element by the Marxist element, gradually change the false con-

---

[1] Explanatory note of the translator [from Chinese to Spanish to French].

sciousness into a true consciousness, so that the Catholics will eventually destroy of their own accord and on their own account, the divine images which they themselves had created. That is our line of action in the struggle for victory against the counter-revolutionary Catholic Church.

Furthermore, we will present a program of tactics applied with success in the Chinese People's Republic in order to liberate the Chinese people from the influence of the Imperialist Catholic Church of Rome.

The Church and its faithful must be induced to take part in the People's government so that the masses may exert their influence on them. The Church cannot be permitted to preserve its supra-national character which places it above the will of the masses. Within the People's government a Bureau in charge of religious affairs and organizations must be created. By imposing on the Church the processes of Democratic centralism the road is being opened through the instrumentality of the masses, to patriotic measures which will weaken the Church and reverse its prestige. This Bureau will organize national, regional, and local associations which will group the Catholics into patriotic organisms. Each association will manifest its submission to the laws of the nation, and its will to observe them.

When these associations have been created and have professed their submission to the laws of the nation, that is when the reactionaries and counter-revolutionists will come forth. These counter-revolutionists, risen from within the Catholic Church, are the first to be rooted up with determination, without, however, the use of force. In any event, the measures taken must be in accordance with the law. Counter-revolutionary aspirations, by their very nature, lead to actions against the government. This principle indicates to us what kind of laws must be applied against those who protest. They must be regarded as unpatriotic criminals who follow the imperialist instructions [directives] issued by the headquarters of the Catholic Church, by Vatican City.

During this phase, the masses will experience a psychological conflict because, on the one hand, they will feel loyalty toward the Church and the Clergy, and, on the other hand, their patriotism will push them to support the People's Government. This conflict should be explored and studied with attention. If one acts precipitously without keeping in mind the acuteness of this psychological conflict, one risks isolating [alienating] the sympathy of these masses. If the bonds between the masses and the Church are very close, the principle of two steps forward and one step backward should be followed. In taking the step backward the People's government must state that it is defending religious freedom and that by the will of the masses, it is establishing reform committees in the associations so that the patriotic masses may express themselves more directly in the leadership of the affairs of the Church.

Let us be vigilant! The Party militants must direct the work of the reform committees. They must eliminate the reactionaries who will be found among the masses. For this job, these slogans must be followed: it is patriotic to adhere to the government and to observe the laws; disobedience is unpatriotic; the associations must profess their patriotism; the unpatriotic elements must be eliminated from the associations and judged as criminals by the masses; for it is the duty of every citizen to punish the criminals. The militants must turn the masses against the criminal elements. As soon as the masses have condemned the criminals and have eliminated them from the associations, they must be judged under the provisions of the laws of the People's government. At the same time, the associations will have to again profess their submission to the laws and make efforts to discover hidden counter-revolutionary activities among their members.

Though the reactionaries have been discovered, the psychological conflict among the masses must continue. It is important that the ecclesiastical authorities and the leaders of the Church should assure them that religion has become purer now that it has been freed from criminal and unpatriotic elements. Our militants who are members of these associations have the important task to cause the leaders of the Church to make these declarations. Of course, during this phase, other disagreements will arise. If one acts arbitrarily one will lose the control over the movement of the masses. The People's government must push in depth [to the utmost] the discussion of all disagreements. During these discussions, care should be taken to discover the counter-revolutionists who had previously gone unnoticed. During this phase, as in the one preceding it, the same slogans are called for: it is patriotic to observe the laws; disobedience is unpatriotic and criminal. The masses must also be informed of the results of conversations between the State and the Church, as well as of the patriotic renaissance of the religious masses in the process of taking the place of [divesting themselves of] decadent, imperialist, and unpatriotic sentiments. With the exception of spiritual affairs, every indication or expression of liaison with Vatican City will have to be spurned as being motivated by imperialist interests and supporting counter-revolutionary activities. The experience in the [our] brother [sister] countries proves that the Catholic Church has always sustained counter-revolutionary activities. Considering the universal scope of the Catholic Church, these experiences constitute irrefragable [irrefutable] proof its conspiracy. During this phase, Vatican City may be expected to voice protests against our campaign. These protests must be utilized as further evidence of the conspiracy of the Church under the direction of Vatican City.

This leads us to the next phase in our attack; its object is the liaison which exists between the Church and Vatican City. It must be anticipated that in the course of the attack the clergy will react violently because it feels it has been struck at its point of support [foundations] and at the very source of its power. It [the Church] must be reminded that its protests against the attacks, of which it is the object because of its attachment to the Vatican, are unpatriotic and against the laws and the State. It must also be made to feel that what it incarnates is unpatriotic. It is the task of our militants to convince the masses that the individual may have his religion, without Vatican City directing the affairs of all Churches of the world. Our militants must also explain the principle of coexistence of patriotism and religion. Thus, those who follow the orders of the Vatican will be ousted from the masses, thus opening the road for the establishment of an independent Church.

A preparatory campaign must be made before a Church may be proclaimed independent. The clerics who cannot be persuaded to submit to the will of the government will be denounced before the masses. Their protests will be used to destroy their influence on the masses. The best tactic [to be followed] for this [purpose] will be to do a simple and anonymous job. Our militants must bring denunciations against these persons. History abounds in proof [examples] as to the possibility of legal action [action at law] against those who are opposed to a separation of the Church and the Vatican. During this phase all necessary arguments must be compiled to convince the Catholic intellectuals that breaking with the Vatican is a step forward, not a step backward. The provisions of the law protecting all religions, and the history of the different protestant [protesting?—protest?] movements will help convince these intellectuals. At the same time, it will be the task of our militants to lead the Catholic associations into a comprehensive movement, requesting the People's government for authorization to establish an independent Church in order to remove from the Catholic associations any unpatriotic stain caused by elements still attached to the Vatican. The People's government will give the authorization, and the independent Church will be organized. It must be kept in mind that the break between the Catholic Church and the Vatican is of importance only for the theologians. The masses, in practicing their religion, are only weakly linked with the Vatican.

And now we have come to the last stage. The separation of Church and Vatican having been consummated, we can proceed to consecrating the leaders of the Church chosen by us. This will arouse the loud protest of the Vatican and major excommunication. It must be made clear that the struggle is carried on away from the faithful and in no way from within their midst [from without and not from within the group of believers]. The Catholic associations will continue to operate, and the masses will be encouraged to practice their religion in the new Church. If one acts with tact and wisdom [if tact and wisdom are applied], one will not destroy the liturgy and the masses will notice only slight differences in the new Church; the protests of the Vatican against the consecration of bishops will reach only the hierarchy of the Church, and the People's government will take charge of rejecting the complaints of the Vatican. Thus, the "old guard" of the Vatican will gradually be isolated. So isolated, action against it will become more and more legal; for it will feel a violent need for protest and playing the martyr. As a result of this attitude, it can only compromise itself by unpatriotic actions.

Though our struggle against the Catholic Church may be victorious, we must use [the force of] persuasion toward the rear-guard of the clergy. This moderate attitude will make the masses understand that the People's Government is truly anxious to guarantee freedom of religion to everyone. And, at the same time, the protesters are ranked with those who are opposed to the feelings of the people and the government.

Once the key posts of the clergy are in our hands and submitted to the People's Government, one will proceed to progressively eliminating from the liturgy those elements which are incompatible with the People's Government. The first changes will affect the sacraments and the prayers. Then, the masses will be protected against all pressure and all obligation to put in an appearance in the church, to practice religion, or to organize associations of whatever religious group.[2] We know full well that when the practice of religion becomes no more than an individual responsibility, it is slowly forgotten. New generations will follow the old, and religion will be no more than an episode of the past, worthy of being dealt with in the history [books] of the World Communist Movement.

Translated by ELIZABETH HANUNIAN,
Legislative Reference Service, Library of Congress.

TRANSLATION (Russian)

APPEAL

OF THE PARTICIPANTS OF THE ALL-UNION CONFERENCE OF THE RELATIVES OF PRISONERS OF THE CHURCH OF ECHB [EVANGELICAL CHRISTIAN BAPTISTS] IN THE U.S.S.R.

To all EChB, saints and faithful in Jesus Christ: Happiness and peace to you from God our Father and God Jesus Christ.

Beloved Brothers and Sisters, St. Paul, in his epistle to the Philippians wrote: "* * * my bonds in Christ are manifest in all the palace" and that "the things that happened unto me have fallen out rather unto the furtherance of the gospel." (*Phil. 1: 12–13*.)

It happened to St. Paul in the first century, but today, it is happening with our relatives and ourselves, although it is now the 20th century.

We, the relatives of prisoners, also want that what happens to us may serve the furtherance of the work of God and, therefore, we want that the imprisonments of our relatives become known to all of you so that you may be participants in that body about which it is said: that it is "fitly joined together and compacted by that which every joint supplieth." (*Eph. 4: 16*.)

Apostle Paul asked the servant of the Christ's Church, Timothy: "Be not thou ashamed of the testimony of our Lord, nor of me, his prisoner." (*II Tim. 1: 8*.) "Remember my bonds", he asked the Church in his letter to the Colossians. (*Col. 4: 18*.)

At this time, your own brothers and sisters beg of you: "Be not ashamed of us, remember our bonds."

We thank God for you, that, due to your serving Him, we, though persecuted by the world, are not left alone and, through you, God in his word, satisfies our needs. And we ask you that, in your prayers to God, you always remember your brothers and sisters in prisons.

How sad it is to read about the case Prophet Jeremiah (*Jer. 38: 15–13*): The only man who remembered the bonds of the Prophet who was in a dungeon, was the heathen Ebed-melech, the Egyptian, but of the people of Israel for whom Prophet Jere niah had shed tears (*Jer. 9: 1*) and whom he wished all the best with all his heart, nobody remembered his sufferings in the dungeon. Today, the blood of Jesus Christ, our Lord, united us in one body and, therefore, if one member suffers, the whole body suffers; when one member is praised, the whole body is praised with him.

We wish to suffer jointly and to enjoy jointly the comforting of Christ, and all the Saints who constitute the Church of God and Christ!

Therefore, if there is someone else who is in a similar situation as we are, having brothers, husbands or sons imprisoned for the word of God, let us know about them and we shall notify the Church.

The Church, in its prayers, will convey the message to its Head, Jesus Christ, who will soon send his protection.

Our Lord is not indifferent to the sufferings of His Church, as the scripture says: "What toucheth you, toucheth the apple of His eye."

---

[2] [In Spanish:] "Then the masses will be protected against constraint and pressure to attend church, to practice religion, or to organize collective groups representing whatever religious sect."

Therefore we shall not hide our sufferings from the Lord in the face of His Church. We shall say, with Paul the Apostle, that we, too, boast of our sorrows (*Rom. 5: 23*). We also want to share with you the sorrows which we, the mothers bear, as our children were taken away from us.

Loving them and following the word of God, that the "future generations to which children will be born" may know (*Ps. 78: 4–7*) and also having received a direct command of God (*Heb. 6: 4*), we brought up and educated our children according to God's teaching. For this, we were separated from our children.

Only you can fully conceive this sorrow, as you are the members of one living body of the Church of Christ, which is also threatened with such participation [in suffering].

We implore you, our brothers and sisters, in our Lord, Jesus Christ and in the love of the Spirit, to rise with us in your prayers to God for our relatives who are in prisons, listed in the information we are herewith enclosing as well as for us and our children.

God bless you!

Yours in Christ, brothers and sisters, relatives of prisoners for the word of God.

At the direction of the All-Union Conference of relatives of the prisoners, EChB in the U.S.S.R.

FEBRUARY 23, 1964

1. GOVORUN (Smolensk)
2. IASTREBOVA (Kharkov)
3. RUDNEVA (Semipalatinsk).

REPORT

ON THE ACTIVITIES OF ALL-UNION CONFERENCE OF RELATIVES OF THE PRISONERS, ECHB, AS OF FEBRUARY 23, 1964

On February 23, 1964, the All-Union Conference of relatives of the prisoners, EChB, took place, which conducted its business according to the following agenda:

AGENDA

OF THE ALL-UNION CONFERENCE OF RELATIVES OF THE PRISONERS SENTENCED FOR THE WORD OF GOD

1. Collection and specification of information concerning the prisoners, EChB, sentenced during the period from 1961 through February 1964, at the time of the introduction of the "New Statute" of the All-Union EChB.

2. Establishing: For what reason and on what charge were sentenced our relatives, brothers and sisters who are now in prisons and in places of deportation.

3. Establishing: for what reasons children are being taken away from believing parents.

4. Our relation, as relatives of prisoners, to officials and authorities.

5. Our service, as relatives of sentenced persons, to the Church and our service to God in our families.

THE COURSE OF THE CONFERENCE

The All-Union Conference of Relatives of Prisoners, remembering the words of the Holy Scripture (*Heb. 13: 3*), studied the reports which arrived from local Churches concerning the prisoners, EChB, sentenced during the period of 1961 through February 1964, edited them and established the following:

1. Full reports were received concerning 102 prisoners.

2. Supplementary information (incomplete) were later received concerning 53 prisoners.

3. Total number of prisoners is 155 persons.

4. Out of this number, 10 persons were released after serving their time or for other reasons.

5. Four persons died during the investigation, before trial and after trial, in prisons and camps.

6. The total number of persons in prisons as of February 1964 (as to which reports were received) was 141 persons.

7. The number of dependents in the families of the prisoners is 297.

8. Of this number, 228 persons were children of preschool and school age.

9. The oldest prisoner is: Arend, Iu. V.—76 years of age.

10. The youngest prisoner is: Gorfeld, G. G.—23 years.

11. Families sentenced: Lozovyi—father, mother, son; Shornikov—father and mother, children of school age were placed in institutions, etc.

The conference studied the question as to the reasons why our relatives, brothers and sisters were sentenced and came to the following unanimous conclusion:

1. All 155 prisoners, EChB, were sentenced not for violations of law or crimes against society or the state, but for their religious belief, for the Word of God, in defiance of the existing laws of our country.

2. The reason for their arrests and trials was the introduction in 1960 of the "New Statute" of the All-Union EChB and their dissatisfaction with it.

This is supported by the analysis of the trials. Thus, for example:

(1) The sentence of the People's Court of the Zmyiskii Region, Province of Kharkov, of May 1, 1962, in the case against Sirokhin, E. M., declares: "The reactionary character of the illegal community headed by the defendant in the village of Sokolovo, is implied in the fact that it [the community] expressed its dissatisfaction with the existing Statute of the 'All-Union EChB, and also in the activities of its executive organ.'"

(2) In the writ of indictment in the case versus Subbotin, F. I., Khmara N. K. et al. (village of Kulunda, Altaislii Krai) it is written:

"Under the pretext of performing religious services and executing religious rites, he committed acts directed towards the criticism of the officially valid Statute of the All-Union EChB", and it is written in the sentence in the same case (Case No. 2–142, of 27 Dec. 1963), that a group of believers, under the disguise of "purification" conducted propaganda against the All-Union Soviet [Council] of EChB and its Statute.

The conference also considered the question of children taken away from parents, EChB, and established that the reports were received concerning five families from which nine children were taken away. It was found that the reason for the taking away of the children was their religious upbringing in their families. The Conference noted that, both, according to the Word of God, and the laws of our country, those believing EChB, has the right of bringing up their children in religious spirit. This is stated in the Decree on the Separation of the Church from the state of 1918, Art. 9: "The citizens can teach and learn religion in a private way," and in the "Convention on the fight against the discrimination in the field of education" Art. 5, p. 6, approved by the Presidium of the Supreme Soviet U.S.S.R. on July 2, 1962, and entered into force on November 1, 1962: "Parents and, in appropriate cases, legal guardians, should have the possibility to ensure religious and moral education of their children according to their own convictions."

The Conference noted that, in connection with such numerous persecutions and oppressions of the believing EChB for the faith in God, in some of them a feeling of hostility toward their persecutors might appear.

The Conference deems it necessary to remind all faithful that they should not admit the feeling of hostility toward the oppressors and should pray for those accusing and persecuting them. (*Matt: 5:44*.)

In the question of our serving the Church as relatives of those jailed for the Word of God, the Conference passed a resolution establishing a Temporary Council of Relatives of the Imprisoned EChB, set down its objectives and tasks, and elected [members of] the Temporary Council.

OBJECTIVES AND TASKS OF THE TEMPORARY COUNCIL OF RELATIVES OF IMPRISONED EVANGELICAL CHRISTIAN BAPTISTS [EChB]

1. Continuous information to the Church of EChB on the EChB imprisoned for the Word of God and on the children taken away from EChB parents, and calling for prayers for the prisoners and the children.

2. Petitioning the Government for the review of all court cases concerning the believing EChB sentenced for the Word of God since 1962, with the purpose of setting them free and fully rehabilitating them; also petitioning the Government for the return to their families of children taken away from their parents.

3. In order to fulfill the tasks set forth under 1 and 2 above, the Council shall keep complete record and files of all information concerning all imprisoned EChB, sentenced for the Word of God, and concerning all children taken away from their parents, EChB, for religious education.

4. Members of the Council can only be members of the Church of EChB, who have relatives, EChB, imprisoned for the Word of God in the U.S.S.R. The members of the Council shall be elected at the All-Union Conferences of Relatives of Imprisoned EChB.

The Conference directs the Temporary Council of Relatives of prisoners to select from among themselves representatives for a personal visit with the Head of the Government and for submitting to him the Appeal of the All-Union Conference of Relatives of Prisoners.

The Conference decided to turn to the whole EChB Church Community in our country with a special appeal asking for prayers for the prisoners and for the children taken away from the believing EChB for education according to the Word of God; and to publish the information concerning the prisoners, EChB, and concerning the children taken away from parents, EChB.

CONFERENCE OF THE TEMPORARY COUNCIL OF RELATIVES OF IMPRISONED ECHB, SENTENCED TO THE WORD OF GOD

1. The Conference of the Temporary Council considered the question of the representative of the Council for visiting of the Head of the Government, and selected from among themselves a delegation composed of three persons:

GOVORUN (of Smolensk)
IASTREBOVA (Kharkov)
RUDNOVA (Semipalatinsk).

The Temporary Council turns to the whole Church and to all believers, EChB, with request:

(a) To submit to the Council full information on all EChB, imprisoned for the Word of God, who are not listed in the published record. Also we ask them to send us corrections and supplementary information on imprisoned EChB, if errors or incomplete information are contained in the record.

(b) To send to the Council information concerning the children taken away [from their parents] for religious education and concerning all court decisions in such matters.

(c) To send to the Council information concerning freed brothers and sisters along with the reasons of release.

(d) Send to the Council information concerning all brothers and sisters who died during [police] investigation, court procedure as well after the trial, in prisons, camps or places of deportation.

". . . They had trial of mockings and scourgings, yea, moreover of bonds and imprisonment." (*Heb. 11: 36.*)

"Remember them that are in bonds, as bound with them." (*Heb. 13: 3.*)

INFORMATION

ON ECHB IMPRISONED FOR THE WORD OF GOD AT THE TIME OF THE INTRODUCTION OF "NEW STATUTE OF THE ALL-UNION ECHB"

Explanation of Abbreviated Chart Items

(for the period 1961 through February, 1964)

In column 4 (section of criminal code under which the person was sentenced) "Ukase" means Ukase (decree) of the Presidium of the Supreme Soviet of the Russian SFSR of May 4, 1961, or the Ukase of the Presidium of the Supreme Soviet of the U.S.S.R. of July 2, 1961.

Sec. 227—means the section of the Criminal Code of the Russian SFSR.
Sec. 209—means the section of the Criminal Code of the Ukrainian SSR.
Sec. 222—means the section of the Criminal Code of the Byelorussian SSR.
Sec. 200—means the section of the Criminal Code of the Kazakh SSR.
In column 5 (term of the sentence).
5d means five years of deportation.
5c means five years of [prison] camp.
5cs means five years of [prison] camp with strict regime.
5cs+3d means five years of [prison] camp with strict regime plus three years of [subsequent] deportation.

RUSSIAN SSR

No.	Last name, first name, patronymic	Date of arrest or trial	Section under which sentenced	Term of sentence	Place of residence before arrest, number of dependents	Remarks
1	2	3	4	5	6	7

Province of Moscow

No.	Last name, first name, patronymic	Date of arrest or trial	Section under which sentenced	Term of sentence	Place of residence before arrest, number of dependents	Remarks
1	Smirnov, V. Ia.	1961	Ukase	5d	Dedovsk, wife, 6 children.	
2	Ryzhuk, V. F.	1961	Ukase	5d	Nakhabino, wife, 3 children.	
3	Rumachik, P. V.	1961	Ukase	5d	Dedovsk, wife, 3 children.	
4	Aleksandrov, P. V.	1961	Ukase	5d	Dedovsk.	
5	Kaiukov, L. L.	1961	Ukase	5d	Dedovsk.	

Province of Tula

No.	Last name, first name, patronymic	Date of arrest or trial	Section under which sentenced	Term of sentence	Place of residence before arrest, number of dependents	Remarks
6	Altrekhov, M. T.	1961	Ukase	5d	Wife.	
7	Iakimenkev, P. A.	1961	Ukase	5d	St. Uzlovaia.	

Province of Smolensk

No.	Last name, first name, patronymic	Date of arrest or trial	Section under which sentenced	Term of sentence	Place of residence before arrest, number of dependents	Remarks
8	Shalypin, D. A.	1963	227	5cs +5d	Demidov, wife, 5 children, mother.	Wife died in 1964.
9	Radionov, P. T.	1963	227	3c	Demidov, 2 children.	

Province of Belgorod

No.	Last name, first name, patronymic	Date of arrest or trial	Section under which sentenced	Term of sentence	Place of residence before arrest, number of dependents	Remarks
10	Nefedov, A.P.	1963	Ukase	5d	Bokhovetc, wife.	
11	Azarov, M. I.	1963	Ukase	5d	Belgorod, wife, 3 children.	
12	Syromiatnikov, D.G.	1963	Ukase	5d	Laptevka, wife, 7 children.	
13	Gubarev,V	1963	Ukase	5d	Gasmishchevo, wife, 4 children.	

Province of Rostov

No.	Last name, first name, patronymic	Date of arrest or trial	Section under which sentenced	Term of sentence	Place of residence before arrest, number of dependents	Remarks
14	Baturyn, N. G.	1962	227	5d	Shakhty, wife, mother, 4 children.	
15	Shostenko, G. F.	1963	227	2d	Rostov, wife.	
16	Rogozhin, Ia. S.	1963	227	4d	Rostov, wife.	

North Ossetia ASSR

No.	Last name, first name, patronymic	Date of arrest or trial	Section under which sentenced	Term of sentence	Place of residence before arrest, number of dependents	Remarks
17	Brykov, M. I.	1961	Ukase	5d	Ordzhonikidzo	

Mari ASSR

No.	Last name, first name, patronymic	Date of arrest or trial	Section under which sentenced	Term of sentence	Place of residence before arrest, number of dependents	Remarks
18	Kozlov, B. I.	1961	Ukase	5d	Ioshkar-Ola, wife, 6 children.	
19	Vinokurov, N. M.	1962	Ukase	5d	Volzhsk, wife, 6 children.	

Tatar ASSR

No.	Last name, first name, patronymic	Date of arrest or trial	Section under which sentenced	Term of sentence	Place of residence before arrest, number of dependents	Remarks
20	Kuksenko, Iu. F.	1961	Ukase	5d	Kazan, wife, 4 children.	
21	Merkulov, V. V.	1963	227	5c	Kazan, mother.	
22	Savin, I. V	1963	227	5c	Kazan, wife, 4 children.	
23	Terentiev, A.	1963	227	5c	Kazan, wife, mother, 3 children.	
24	Kuzmicheva, N.	1963	227	5c	Kazan.	
25	Akhmetvaleeva, Lidia.	1963	227	5c	Kazan, mother.	

RUSSIAN SSR—Continued

No.	Last name, first name, patronymic	Date of arrest or trial	Section under which sentenced	Term of sentence	Place of residence before arrest, number of dependents	Remarks
1	2	3	4	5	6	7

Province of Omsk

No.	Last name, first name, patronymic	Date of arrest or trial	Section under which sentenced	Term of sentence	Place of residence before arrest, number of dependents	Remarks
26	Troian, B. G.	1963	227	5d	Ust-Ishim, wife, 5 children.	
27	Khoroshenko, M. K.	1963	227	5d	Ust-Ishim, wife, 1 child.	
28	Sadonikov, S. A.	1963	227	5d	Ust-Ishim, wife, 1 child.	
29	Disenko, I. U.	1963	227	5d	Tevriz, wife.	
30	Kasler, D. I.	1963	227	5d	Tevriz, wife, 4 children.	
31	Kovalev, P. G.	1961	Ukase	2d	Omekh.	Released, 1963.

Province of Novosibirsk

No.	Last name, first name, patronymic	Date of arrest or trial	Section under which sentenced	Term of sentence	Place of residence before arrest, number of dependents	Remarks
32	Miroshnychenko, I. M.	1962	227	5d	Kozharka, wife, 2 children.	
33	Belotserkovskii, L. A.	1962	227	5d	Ponomarevka, wife.	
34	Zel. L. B.	1962	227	5d	Pikhtovka, wife, 5 children.	
35	Lvova, Nadezhda	1962	227	5d	Novosibirsk, 1 child.	
36	Bannikov, G.	1962	227	5d	Pikhtovka, wife.	

Province of Kemerovo

No.	Last name, first name, patronymic	Date of arrest or trial	Section under which sentenced	Term of sentence	Place of residence before arrest, number of dependents	Remarks
37	Kroker, K. K.	1962	227	5d	Mezhdurechensk, wife, 7 children.	
38	Shiva, P. V.	1962	227	5d	Tashtagol, wife, 3 children.	
39	Vedel, I. I.	1962	227	5d	Iurga, wife, 6 children.	
40	Keiatungen, V.	1963	227	5d	Mezhdurechensk.	

Altai Region [Krai]

No.	Last name, first name, patronymic	Date of arrest or trial	Section under which sentenced	Term of sentence	Place of residence before arrest, number of dependents	Remarks
41	Minipov, D. V.	1962	226	5cs	Barnaul, wife, 4 children.	
42	Mikhalkov, Iu. I.	1962	226	3c	Barnaul, wife, 1 child.	
43	Lebedev, G. D.	1962	226	4cs	Barnaul, wife.	
44	Budemir, I. M.	1962	227	2c	Barnaul, wife, 5 children.	
45	Shvertcer, A. A.	1962	227	5cs	Barnaul.	
46	Subbotin, F. I.	1963	227	5c	Kulunda, wife, 8 children.	
47	Khmara, V. K.	1963	227	3c	Kulunda, wife, 5 children.	
48	Khmara, Nikolai, K.	1963	227	3c	Kulunda, wife, 4 children.	Jan. 9, 1964, died in the prison at Barnaul.
49	Iantc, N. Ia.	1963	227	3d	Slavgorod, wife.	

Prinorskii Krai

No.	Last name, first name, patronymic	Date of arrest or trial	Section under which sentenced	Term of sentence	Place of residence before arrest, number of dependents	Remarks
50	Lavrinov, V. S.	1961	Ukase	5d	Spasskii Region.	

UKRAINE

Province of Khmelnitskii

No.	Last name, first name, patronymic	Date of arrest or trial	Section under which sentenced	Term of sentence	Place of residence before arrest, number of dependents	Remarks
51	Morozovskii, V. I.	1962	209	3c	Khmelnitskii.	
52	Levchuk, A. N.	1962	209	5c+5d	Khmelnitskii.	
53	Levchuk, Ts. N.	1962	209	4c+4d	Khmelnitskii.	
54	Cavchuk, F. N.	1962	209	3c	Shepetovka, mother.	

UKRAINE—Continued

No.	Last name, first name, patronymic	Date of arrest or trial	Section under which sentenced	Term of sentence	Place of residence before arrest, number of dependents	Remarks
1	2	3	4	5	6	7

Province of Khmelnitskii—Continued

55	Tymoshchuk, S. K.	1962	209	5c	Pashchuki, wife, 9 children.	
56	Graboshchuk, A. M.	1962	209	3c	Vovkivchyki, wife, 2 children.	
57	Benishchuk, K. F.	1962	209	3c	Vovkivchyki, wife, 2 children.	
58	Shevchuk, P. D.	1963	209	2c	Pecheski, wife, mother-in-law, 8 children.	
59	Bartolomei, I. N.	1962	209	3.5c	Slavuta, wife, 4 children.	

Province of Rovno

60	Kovalchuk, A. of Rovno, was under police investigation from January 1962 to July 1962, for the Word of God; as a result, he lost his health. At the present time lives at home, as a disabled person of the first group.

Province of Chernigov

61	Voronenka, P. A.	1964	Ukase	2.5d	Staraia Iurkobiga, wife.	

Province of Cherkassy

62	Shepel, N.	1964	209		Cherkassy, mother.	
63	Chesenko, B.	1964	209		Cherkassy	Both under investigation.

Province of Kirovograd

64	Leshchenko, Anna	1962	209	3c	Kirovograd	
65	Bondarenka, V. D.	1962	209	5c+5d	Kirovograd, wife, 3 children.	
66	Glukhoi, L. A.	1962	209	5c+5d	Kirovograd, mother, grandmother.	

Province of Odessa

67	Bondarenko, I. D.	1962	209	5c+3d	Odessa, mother, father.	
68	Shevchenko, N. P.	1962	209	4c	Odessa, wife.	

Province of Nikolaev

69	Kuchenenko, Nikolai Samoilovich, on July 22, 1962, died during police investigation at Nikolaev; left wife

Province of Donets

70	Prokofiev, A. F.	1962	209	5cs+5d	Volnovaia	
71	Pugariova, Taissa	1964	209	4c	Nikitovka	
72	Khloponina, Evgenia.	1964	209	4c	Nikitovka	
73	Popov, Al. Iar.	1964	209	5c	Nikitovka, wife, 4 children.	
74	Ribalka, V.	1964	209	5c	Nikitovka, wife, 5 children.	

UKRAINE—Continued

No.	Last name, first name, patronymic	Date of arrest or trial	Section under which sentenced	Term of sentence	Place of residence before arrest, number of dependents	Remarks
1	2	3	4	5	6	7

Province of Kharkov

No.	Last name, first name, patronymic	Date of arrest or trial	Section under which sentenced	Term of sentence	Place of residence before arrest, number of dependents	Remarks
75	Lozovoi, A. D	1961	Ukase	5d	Kharkov	
76	Lozovoi, V. A	1961		1.5 comp. treatment.	Kharkov	Released 1963.
77	Streltsov, A	1961		1.5 comp. treatment.	Kharkov, wife, 4 children.	Released 1963.
78	Zdorovets, B. M	1961	Sec. 62	5cs+3d	Olshany, wife, 4 children.	
79	Mosha, V. K	1961	209	3c	Kharkov, father, mother.	
80	Lozovaia, Martha	1961	Ukase	3d	Kharkov	
81	Sirokhin, E. M	1962	209	3c	Sokolovo, wife, 5 children.	
82	Shornik, P. S	1963	209	2c	Protopopovka, 2 children.	
83	Shornik, Agrippina	1963	209	3c	Protopopovka	
84	Krivko, M	1961	209	1.5c	Merefa, wife	
85	Korobka, Anna, P	1963	209	3c	Dergachi, wife, 2 children.	Interned.
86	Iastrebov, V. S	1963	209	5c + 5d	Dergachi, wife, 4 children.	
87	Movchan, V	1963	209	3c	Kharkov, wife, 4 children.	

BYELORUSSIA

Province of Brest

No.	Last name, first name, patronymic	Date of arrest or trial	Section under which sentenced	Term of sentence	Place of residence before arrest, number of dependents	Remarks
88	Matveiuk, S. A	1963	222	5c	Brest, wife, 3 children.	
89	Shepetunko, G. N	1963	222	5c	Brest, wife, 6 children.	
90	Kotovich, I. A	1963	222	4c	Brest, wife.	
91	Fedorchuk, E. Ia	1963	222	3c	Brest, wife, 2 children.	
92	Antonenko, V. I	1962	222	5c	Minsh	
93	Makarenko, G. M	1962	222	2c	Minsh	
94	Pilipenko, A. P	1963	222	3c	Minsh	

KAZAKHSTAN

Province of Semipalatinsk

No.	Last name, first name, patronymic	Date of arrest or trial	Section under which sentenced	Term of sentence	Place of residence before arrest, number of dependents	Remarks
95	Rudnev, V. T	1962	200	5cs	Semipalatinsk, wife, 8 children.	
96	Kribasheev, N	1962	200	5cs	Semipalatinsk, wife, 7 children.	
97	Gofeld, G. G	1962	200	5cs		
98	Plit, A. G	1962	200	1c		Released in 1963. Old man, born 1888.
99	Arend, Iu. V	1963	200	1c	Semipalatinsk, wife.	
100	Altukhov, I. I	1962		5cs	Semipalatinsk, wife.	

Province of Alma-Ata

No.	Last name, first name, patronymic	Date of arrest or trial	Section under which sentenced	Term of sentence	Place of residence before arrest, number of dependents	Remarks
101	Shtefin, Ts. P	1964	200	5cs	Issyk, wife, 3 children.	
102	Klassen, A. P	1964	200	4c	Issyk, wife, 5 children.	

Full information was received concerning 102 prisoners.

In addition to the above listed persons, according to incomplete data, there were sentenced for the Word of God during the period of 1961 to February 1964:

1. Province of Kursk—12 persons.
2. North Ossetia, Auton. SSR.—one person, Gernikov, N. K.
3. Tatar, ASSR—one person, Renina, Elena.
4. Province of Perm—seven persons (10 dependents) including Novozhilov, L.S. and Starkov, M.G.
5. Province of Novorossiisk—one person, Latyshev, A.
6. Province of Sumi—three persons (seven dependents): Zikunov, I. E., Nalivaiko Ia. M., Soloshenko, Ia. Ia.
7. Province of Crimea—one person, Shozsa, P.M.
8. Province of Vitebsk—three persons.
9. Province of Karaganda—two persons: Bibe, Otto Pete (died in jail on January 30, 1964), Klassen David, Ivanovich.
10. Province of Kokchetav—two persons, Koon, father and Koon, son.
11. Province of Tselingrad—eight persons (22 dependents), Soloviev, P.P., Parishev, V. Ia., Sharanov, M., Babich, T.T., Lapaev, Maks, Fed. (died in jail in 1963), Boiko, L., Nesredov, F. F., Baziliuk, P.
12. Azerbaijan, SSR—one person, Sabeliev, S.I. of Baku.
13. Kirghiz SSR—one person, Ballikh, Ia. I., of Kant (?).
14. Uzbek SSR—10 persons, including: Khranov, N. P., of Tashkent, and Avetisov V. of Iange-Iul. Of them five persons were released.

INFORMATION concerning children taken away by court order from their EChB parents for religious education:

1. Goncharov Mikola (?)—15 years of age, Province of Smolensk, Pochetkovskii Region, trial in April, 1963.
2. Goncharova Masha—12 years, same as above.
3. Goncharov, Vania—8 years, same as above.
4. Govorun Seriozha—5 years, of Smolensk, trial in December, 1963.
5. Renina, girl—14 years, of Kazan, trial in 1962.
6. Zhornikova Halia—12 years, Province of Kharkov, Dergachevskii Region, village of Olshany, trial in 1963.
7. Zhornikov, Seriozha—9 years, same as above.
8. Korobka, Boria—13 years, of Dergachi, trial on November 26, 1963.
9. Korobka, Tola—7 years, same as above.

Translated by GEORGE STAROSOLSKY,
Legislative Reference Service, Library of Congress.

TRANSLATION (Russian)

For the Lord heareth the poor, and despiseth not His prisoners (*Ps. 68: 34*) [*Ps. 69: 33?*]

TO THE BRETHREN AND SISTERS, EVANGELICAL CHRISTIAN BAPTISTS, WHO COMPOSE THE CHURCH OF CHRIST IN OUR COUNTRY FROM THE TEMPORARY COUNCIL OF RELATIVES OF THE PRISONERS, EVANGELICAL CHRISTIAN BAPTISTS IN THE U.S.S.R., SENTENCED FOR THE WORD OF GOD

APPEAL

God-loved Children of God!

Again, we wish to give praise and gratitude to our beloved God for your participation in our sufferings the comforts wherewith we are comforted by God (*2 Cor. 1: 7, 1:4*).

For our comfort, God left His word and speaks by the Holy Spirit through Paul, the Apostle: "Comfort one another by these words (*I Thes. 4:18*). We wish to comfort you with the words of the Scripture: "God heareth the poor, and despiseth not His prisoners" (*Ps. 68:34*) [probably *Ps. 69: 33*—Translator]. The Lord also listens to your prayers. We, as well as our prisoners with whom we meet, though not very often can testify to this. Due to your prayers, God gives them so much joy and courage that one of them, when hearing at a meeting about the great awakening among the people of God caused by their bonds, said: "I would be pleased to stay here even my whole life long, if this would bring fruits to the cause of the purification and sanctification of the Church". Such is also the spirit of the other prisoners. To some of our friends, God opened the doors of prisons after the prayers of our Church, so that they may praise Jesus Christ in liberty. This fills us with joy and pleases us because God Himself said: "Ask and ye shall receive, 'that your joy may be full'" (*John, 16: 24*). Yet we do not want to hide this joy from all of you: "that for the gift bestowed upon us by the means of many persons, thanks may be given by many." (*2 Cor. 1: 11.*)

At the same time, we inform you about new prisoners so that you, imitating God as His beloved children, may not neglect His prisoners in your prayers for them as well as for all the matters that they and their families need.

Dearly beloved: We ask you to send information on releases from prison and new imprisonments of our brethren and sisters, to the Council of Relatives of the prisoners, Evangelical Christian Baptists.

Take heart, friends. God is with us in all our fire ordeals. Amen.

THE TEMPORARY COUNCIL OF RELATIVES OF PRISONERS, MEMBERS OF THE CHURCH OF EVANGELICAL CHRISTIAN BAPTISTS

At the direction of the Temporary Council of Relatives of Prisoners—
Members of the Council: 1. RUDNEVA,
2. IASTREBOVA,
3. GOVORUN

JULY 5, 1964.

"They had trial of mockings and scourgings,
yea, moreover of bonds and imprisonment."
(*Heb. 11: 36.*)
"Remember them that are in bonds, as bound
with them." (*Heb. 13: 3*).

INFORMATION

ON THE EVANGELICAL CHRISTIAN BAPTISTS IMPRISONED FOR THE WORD OF GOD AT THE TIME OF THE INTRODUCTION OF THE "NEW STATUTE OF THE ALL-UNION CONFERENCE OF EVANGELICAL CHRISTIAN BAPTISTS" (FOR THE PERIOD FROM 1961 TO JUNE 1964)

LIST No. 2

(CONTINUATION OF THE LIST OF PRISONERS OF FEBRUARY 23, 1964)

Abbreviations of chart items—

In column No. 4 (section under which sentenced):
Ukase—Ukase of the Presidium of the Supreme Soviet of the Russian SFSR of May 4, 1961, or Ukase of the Presidium of the Supreme Soviet of the Ukrainian SSR of July 12, 1961.
Sec. 227—section of the Criminal Code of the Russian SFSR.
Sec. 209—section of the Criminal Code of the Ukrainian SSR.
Sec. 222—section of the Criminal Code of the Byelorussian SSR.
Sec. 220—section of the Criminal Code of the Kazakh SSR.
In column No. 5 (to what term sentenced):
5d—five years of deportation.
5c—five years of [prison] camp.
5cs—five years of [prison] camp with strict regime.
5cs + 3d—five years of [prison] camp with strict regime plus three years of deportation.

RUSSIAN RSFSR

No.	Last name, first name, patronymic	Date of arrest or sentence	Section under which sentenced	Term of sentence	Residence prior to arrest and number of dependents	Remarks
1	2	3	4	5	6	7

Province of Kursk

103	Artivshenko, B. T..	1961	Ukase....	5d.........	Kursk, wife, 4 children.	
104	Arolkin, P. P.......	1961	Ukase....	5d.........	Kursk, wife, 3 children.	
105	Puzanov, I. I.......	1961	Ukase....	5d.........	Kursk, wife, 8 children.	
106	Sogachev, E. E.....	1961	Ukase....	5d.........	Kursk, wife, 3 children.	
107	Onchinnikov, L. D.	1961	Ukase....	3d.........		
108	Shatunov, L. F....	1962	Ukase....	5d.........	Kursk, wife, daughter.	
109	Trufanov, Ia. G....	1961	Ukase....	5d.........	Kursk, 2 dependents.	Free, April 1964.
110	Puzanov, P. I......	1963	Ukase....	5d.........	Kursk, wife, 2 children.	
111	Minaev, N. I.......	1963	Ukase....	5d.........	Kursk, wife, 3 children.	
112	Diumin, N. B......	1963	Ukase....	4d.........	Kursk, wife.........	
113	Sokolov, I. V......	1963	Ukase....	4d.........	Kursk, mother, aunt..	
114	Bykov, M..........	1963	Ukase....	5d.........	Kursk-Province, wife, 3 children.	

Province of Cheliabinsk

115	Fedin, N. P.......	1963	Sec. 227...	5d.........	Kopeisk, wife.......	
116	Nobozhilov, A. S...	1963	Sec. 227...	5d.........	Perm, wife..........	
117	Starkov, M. G......	1962	Ukase....	5d.........	Perm, wife..........	
118	Bolegov, A. E.....	1962	Ukase....	5d.........	Perm...............	
119	Samokhvalov, I. S..	1962	Ukase....	3d.........	Perm...............	
120	Obusova, Evdokia..	1962	Ukase....	5d.........	Perm...............	

Province of Rostov

121	Erisov, D. P.......	1964	Sec. 227...	5d.........	Rostov, wife, 1 son..	
122	Zhevmiruk, V. V...	1964	Sec. 227...	2c.........	Rostov, wife, children.	
123	Inina, A. F........	1964	Ukase.....	5d.........	Novocherkassk......	

Province of Orenburg

124	Peters, D. D.......	1964	Sec. 227...	5d.........	Kortitsa, wife.......	
125	Peters, Ekaterina...	1964	Sec. 227...	5d.........	Kortitsa............	

Province of Kalinograd

126	Sulin, M. A........	1962	Ukase.....	5d.........	Kaliningrad, wife, 4 children.	Released because of sickness, 3/27/64.

Province of Northern Caucasus

127	Ryzhenko...........	1962	Ukase.....	5d.........	Cherkassk..........	Died 1963, at place of deportation.
128	Bezmatnyi..........	1962	Ukase.....	5d.........	Cherkassk, wife.....	
129	Kirilov, I. G.......	1962	Ukase.....	5d.........	Krasnodar-Region, wife, 2 children.	
130	Kobzar, I. S........	1962	Ukase.....	5d.........	Krasnodar-Region, wife, 8 children.	
131	Fenin, I. I.........	1962	Ukase.....	5d.........	Krasnodar-Region, wife, 5 children.	
132	Olkhov, S. F.......	1962	Ukase.....	5d.........	Krasnodar-Region, wife, 5 children.	
133	Samsonenko, F. T..	1963	Ukase.....	5d.........	Novorossiisk........	Released, 1963.

RUSSIAN RSFSR—Continued

No.	Last name, first name, patronymic	Date of arrest or sentence	Section under which sentenced	Term of sentence	Residence prior to arrest and number of dependents	Remarks
1	2	3	4	5	6	7

Tatar Autonomous SSR

| 134 | Suchkov, V. S.____ | 1964 | Sec. 227___ | 3c_____ | Kazan_____ | |

Province of Kemerovo

| 135 | Zakharov, P. F.____ | 1964 | _____ | 3c + 5d___ | Prokopievsk, 3 children. | |

UKRAINE
Province of Sumy

136	Nalivajko, Ia. M.___	1961	Ukase____	4d_____	Sumy Prov., 1 child.	Wife died in 1963.
137	Zykunov, U. E.____	1961	Ukase____	3d_____	Sumy Prov., wife, 5 children.	
138	Soloshenko, Ia. Ia._	1962	Ukase____	5d_____	Lebedinskii Distr., Tokary–B., wife.	

Province of Cherkasy

139	Shokha, N. M.____	1964	Sec. 209__	5c+5d____	Smela, wife_____	
140	Zhuchenko, K. P.__	1964	Sec. 209__	5c_____	Cherkasy_____	
141	Aglicheva, L. D.___	1964	Sec. 209__	5c_____	Smela, 3 children___	

Province of Khmelnitskyi

| 142 | Bortiuk, D. I._____ | 1961 | Ukase____ | 5d_____ | Presluzh, wife, 3 children. | |

BYELORUSSIA
Province of Vitebsk

| 144 | Prokhorenko, F. Ia._ | _____ | Sec. 222___ | 5c+5d____ | Vitebsk, wife, 3 children. | |

UZBEK SSR

145	Neverov, A. I._____	1964	Sec. 141, No. 1.	5c_____	Prov. of Tashkent, wife, 3 children.	
146	Garmashev, B. I.___	1964	Sec. 141, No. 1.	5c_____	Tashkent, wife, 3 children.	
147	Zubov, A. F._____	1964	Sec. 141, No. 1.	5c_____	Tashkent, wife_____	

KAZAKHSTAN
Province of Alma-Ata

| 148 | Wolf, P. I._____ | 1942 | Investigation. | _____ | Isyk, wife, 6 children. | |
| 149 | Esau, Iabov_____ | 1942 | Investigation. | _____ | Isyk, wife, 8 children, aunt. | |

Moldavia

| 150 | Gladkevich, B.____ | _____ | Sec. 143___ | 4c+5d____ | Kishinev_____ | |

1. Information was received concerning 150 prisoners.
2. Additional (incomplete) information was received concerning 47 persons.
3. The total number of prisoners, Evangelical Christian Baptist, sentenced between 1961 and June 1954, is 197 persons.
4. Five people died during the investigation before trial and after the trial in jails and camps.

> ". . . and others were tortured not accepting deliverance that they might obtain a better resurrection." (*Heb. 11:35*)

1. Khmara, N. K. (died on Jan. 9, 1964, in the prison of Barnaul).
2. Kucherenko, K. S. (died during the investigation, Jan. 22, 1962, at Nikolaev).
3. Vibe, O. L. (died in prison on Jan. 30, 1964).
4. Lopaev, M. F. (died in prison in 1963).
5. Ryzhenko (died at the place of deportation, 1963).

5. Out of this number the following persons were released after serving their time or for other reasons:

1. Kovalev, L. G. (of Omsk)
2. Lovalchuk, A. (Rovno)
3. Lozovoi, V. A. (Kharkov)
4. Streltsov A. (Kharkov)
5. Krivko, M. (Kharkov)
6. Arend, Iu. V. (Semipalatinsk)
7. Chernikov, I. K. (Province of Osetinsk)
8. Trufanov, Ia. G. (Kursk)
9. Samokhvalov, I. S. (Perm)
10. Supin, M. A. (Kaliningrad)
11. Khrapov, N. G. (Tashkent)
12. Putinin (Tashkent)
13. Semeriuk (Tashkent)
14. Ogorodnikov (Tashkent)
15. Pumiantsev (Tashkent)
16. Lavrinov (Primorskii Krai)
17. Samsonenko (Novorosiisk)
18. Pigareva, A. T. (Nikitovka)
19. Khlopina, E. (Nikitovka)
20. Popov, A. (Nikitovka)
21. Pybalka (Nikitovka)
22. Brykov, I. I. (Ordzhonikidze)

6. The total number of prisoners in prisons, places of deportation or under investigation is 174 persons.
7. Number of dependents in the families of prisoners—442 persons.
8. Of this number, at preschool and school age—341 persons.
9. Sisters [women] sentenced for the word of God, and under investigation—15 persons.
10. In addition to list No. 1, the following children were taken away from their parents for Christian education and for being faithful Evangelical Christian Baptists:

1. Sirozhina, Lubov, Evgenievna—14 years of age.
2. Sirozhina, Nadezhda, Evgenievna—11 years of age.
3. Sirozhina, Raisa, Evgenievna—9 years old.

They were taken away in April 1964, according to the decision of the Court at Sokolovo, Zmiievskii Region, Province of Kharkov. Their father is a disabled veteran of the Fatherland War, 1st group, blind in both eyes, sentenced for Christian education of his children and for the management of the Church of Evangelical Christian Baptists at Sokolovo, to 3 years of a regular prison camp.

Translated by GEORGE STAROSOLSKY,
Legislative Reference Service, Library of Congress.

INDEX

NOTE.—The Senate Internal Security Subcommittee attaches no significance to the mere fact of the appearance of the name of an individual or an organization in this index.

THE NEW COMMUNIST PROPAGANDA LINE ON RELIGION

HEARING

BEFORE THE

COMMITTEE ON UN-AMERICAN ACTIVITIES
HOUSE OF REPRESENTATIVES

NINETIETH CONGRESS

AUGUST 10, 1967

(INCLUDING INDEX)

Printed for the use of the
Committee on Un-American Activities

II

CONTENTS

III

The House Committee on Un-American Activities is a standing committee of the House of Representatives, constituted as such by the rules of the House, adopted pursuant to Article I, section 5, of the Constitution of the United States which authorizes the House to determine the rules of its proceedings.

RULES ADOPTED BY THE 90TH CONGRESS

House Resolution 7, January 10, 1967

RESOLUTION

Resolved, That the Rules of the House of Representatives of the Eighty-ninth Congress, together with all applicable provisions of the Legislative Reorganization Act of 1946, as amended, be, and they are hereby, adopted as the Rules of the House of Representatives of the Ninetieth Congress * * *

*   *   *   *   *   *   *

RULE X

STANDING COMMITTEES

1. There shall be elected by the House, at the commencement of each Congress

*   *   *   *   *   *   *

(r) Committee on Un-American Activities, to consist of nine Members.

*   *   *   *   *   *   *

RULE XI

POWERS AND DUTIES OF COMMITTEES

*   *   *   *   *   *   *

18. Committee on Un-American Activities.
(a) Un-American activities.
(b) The Committee on Un-American Activities, as a whole or by subcommittee, is authorized to make from time to time investigations of (1) the extent, character, and objects of un-American propaganda activities in the United States, (2) the diffusion within the United States of subversive and un-American propaganda that is instigated from foreign countries or of a domestic origin and attacks the principle of the form of government as guaranteed by our Constitution, and (3) all other questions in relation thereto that would aid Congress in any necessary remedial legislation.

The Committee on Un-American Activities shall report to the House (or to the Clerk of the House if the House is not in session) the results of any such investigation, together with such recommendations as it deems advisable.

For the purpose of any such investigation, the Committee on Un-American Activities, or any subcommittee thereof, is authorized to sit and act at such times and places within the United States, whether or not the House is sitting, has recessed, or has adjourned, to hold such hearings, to require the attendance of such witnesses and the production of such books, papers, and documents, and to take such testimony, as it deems necessary. Subpenas may be issued under the signature of the chairman of the committee or any subcommittee, or by any member designated by any such chairman, and may be served by any person designated by any such chairman or member.

*   *   *   *   *   *   *

27. To assist the House in appraising the administration of the laws and in developing such amendments or related legislation as it may deem necessary, each standing committee of the House shall exercise continuous watchfulness of the execution by the administrative agencies concerned of any laws, the subject matter of which is within the jurisdiction of such committee; and, for that purpose, shall study all pertinent reports and data submitted to the House by the agencies in the executive branch of the Government.

*   *   *   *   *   *   *

SYNOPSIS

A subcommittee of the Committee on Un-American Activities held a public hearing in Washington, D.C., on August 10, 1967, to receive the testimony of the Rev. Richard Wurmbrand.

The hearing was held pursuant to a committee resolution which authorized that hearings be held "relating to the extent and character of Communist propaganda and conspiratorial techniques employed within the United States to promote the objectives of the Communist Party in the United States and to advance the purposes of the world Communist movement by the dissemination of false and misleading information concerning Communist doctrine and practices in regard to religion and ethnic and minority groups."

In his opening statement the chairman cited statements by Lenin and Stalin regarding the traditional Communist position on religion. He also reviewed other Communist statements on the subject:

Sixty-two years ago, Lenin wrote:
" 'Religion is the opium of the people.' Religion is a kind of spiritual vodka in which the slaves of capital drown their human shape and their claims to any decent human life."

Forty years ago, Stalin wrote:
"The [Communist] Party cannot be neutral towards religion. . . . Anti-religious propaganda is a means by which the complete liquidation of the reactionary clergy must be brought about."

In 1946 an official Soviet organ, *Young Bolshevik*, stated:
"Dialectical materialism, the philosophy of Marxism-Leninism and the theoretical foundation of the Communist Party, is incompatible with religion. . . . the [Communist] Party . . . is bound to oppose religion."

Going back to Lenin again, he stated in 1909 that "Marxism is . . . relentlessly hostile to religion."

Earl Browder, for many years the leader of the Communist Party in this country, stated that "the Communist Party is the enemy of religion."

The chairman also noted that as recently as 1964 the Soviet Communist Party had established an Institute of Scientific Atheism to direct an intensified campaign against religious beliefs at every level and in every walk of Soviet life.

The chairman then quoted several recent statements which revealed that Communists had ostensibly reversed their position on religion and were now telling Christians that they can and must work together with Communists to obtain what they call a common goal—a better world for mankind.

The chairman pointed out that:

These recent statements by Communist officials and publications, if sincere, are certainly earth-shaking. If they are genuine, they reflect a major and fundamental change in basic Communist doctrine, a change that could have far-reaching effects in all parts of the world, a change that could reshape the thinking of millions of people on the subject of communism.

The Communists, of course, have made many false and treacherous statements in the past to serve their devious purposes. The 50-year history of their dealings with non-Communists on all levels, governmental and otherwise, is filled with examples of this—calculated, cynically and grossly false statements made by Communists and their agents for no other reason than to mislead non-Communists about the real nature and intent of communism.

507

He asked this question: "Is the new Communist line on religion another example of this, or does it actually indicate a real change in communism?"

Rev. Richard Wurmbrand testified to develop for the record facts which would assist the Congress and the American people in answering that question.

Rev. Wurmbrand is a Lutheran pastor and a native of Rumania. He was imprisoned after the Communist takeover of his country and was released in 1964 as a part of a general amnesty, after having spent 14 years in prison. He arrived in the United States in 1966.

Rev. Wurmbrand produced many letters from prominent clergymen in Europe and in the United States attesting to his reliability. He bears 18 ugly scars on his back, a proof of the physical tortures he had suffered at the hands of the Communist regime in Rumania. The scars, he said, "are not mine; they are signs of the torturing of my fatherland and of my church."

The witness spoke with the knowledge and emotion one might expect from a man who had experienced a Communist takeover of his country and suffered unmercifully at the hands of the oppressors for his religious beliefs.

He said that before the Communists came to power in Rumania, persons who warned what would happen to religion under communism were "besmeared." He also testified that Rumanian churches had been infiltrated prior to the Communist takeover:

Professor Constantinescu Iashi was one of the best known theological professors of Rumania. When the Communists came to power, he became Communist Minister of Culture, a member of the Communist government. People opened their eyes and asked, "But how? You have prepared for ministry thousands of priests. How is it?" He answered, "I have been sent by the Communist Party in the theological seminary."

Bende, the secretary of the Protestant seminary in Cluj in the capitalist times, says that he has been sent by the party there to prepare the students in the radical sense.

When the Communists came to power in Rumania, Orthodox priests, Riosheanu, Patrashcoiu, and others, appeared dressed at once as colonels of the secret police and arrested and beat their parishioners. When the parishioners asked them, "But how is this possible? This is a nightmare. You have been my priest; I kissed your hand; I took the sacraments from you," they answered: "You dupes, you idiots, the Communist Party has sent us in the church."

After his release from prison, Rev. Wurmbrand stated, he was called before the secret police on two occasions and was told: "Now you leave [Rumania]. Preach Christ as much as you like, but don't touch us!" If he spoke against communism, the secret police warned, he would either be shot or kidnaped and returned to Rumania. He said he had known men in prison who had been "brought back," and although he must live with the fear of being forcibly returned to Rumania, he preaches against communism whenever he has the opportunity.

Since his arrival in the United States, Rev. Wurmbrand said he has preached to all religious denominations: "The rank and file believe us, weep when they hear what is happening there * * *." He continued:

When you arrive to the top leaders of churches, some either disbelieve you or ask you, beg you, not to speak.

*   *   *   *   *   *   *

I have been asked, "Well, speak about Christ! We know that you are a very gifted preacher * * *." I was told these very words: "Don't speak against communism, because this will make men hate the Communists and the Russians."

*   *   *   *   *   *   *

Then I asked them, "How is it possible? Please explain it to me. How is it possible that you gave me exactly the same advice as the Communist secret police gave me? They also told me, "Preach Christ and don't speak about communism."

Committee counsel read to Rev. Wurmbrand some of the statements recently made by Communists in their efforts to promote a "dialogue" between themselves and Christians. These statements expressed opposition to religious persecution and coercive methods aimed at religion. They also claimed that the Soviet Union had at no time passed laws to restrict freedom of conscience; that it guarantees religious liberty by law; and that no organ of Soviet power engages in antireligious propaganda.

Commenting on the above declarations, Rev. Wurmbrand testified that before the Communists came to power in Rumania they had "played also the role of being friends of religion."

"Everywhere," he said, "the Communists, until they have the power, say that they are the friends of religion."

Rev. Wurmbrand then produced documentary evidence to show what the Communists do "after they come to power."

Out of "hundreds of documents" he said he had in his possession, Rev. Wurmbrand selected about 20 of the most recent articles from the Soviet press which demonstrated how the alleged "guarantee" of religious freedom works in the Soviet Union. The articles were newspaper reports of trials of persons charged with crimes against the state. In most instances the punishment meted out to individuals who persist in active religious practices is also revealed.

These documents—all published in the Soviet Communist press in 1966 and 1967—revealed that persons had been imprisoned for the following acts:

Showing films of a religious nature to children;
Distributing religious magazines;
Baptizing children;
Teaching religion to children.

Parents who persist in teaching their children about Christ are denied "parental rights"; the children are removed from their care and placed in state schools away from parental influence.

As Rev. Wurmbrand translated articles which told of children being taken from their parents, he was moved almost to the point of tears, saying:

I have known mothers from whom their children have been taken away. In a house which has been full with the noise, with the laughter, with the kicking of children, now there is a great silence of God.
I have seen these mothers; they were like bits of stone. You could not speak with them.
Six children taken away, and that is called "religious liberty," * * *.

The documents translated by Rev. Wurmbrand revealed that brutal suppression and persecution of all religions is still the trademark of communism. These reports of trials and the punishment meted out to those who refuse to deny God were published by the Communists themselves in their government-controlled press. They contradict the statements advanced by such Communist theoreticians as Aptheker, of the United States, and Garaudy, of France, as a basis for a "dialogue" with Christians.

As he finished translating the documents, Rev. Wurmbrand asked:

Now, in matters of communism, who knows communism better? *Pravda*, Kosygin, or Mr. Aptheker, the theoretician of the American Communist Party? Who of these should I believe? Aptheker should go to Mr. Kosygin, and they should convene what they should say.

It is said that witnesses were brought against Jesus at the trial, but what one witness said did not correspond with the other witness. I would recommend to the Communists, when they wish to lie, they should come together and convene how to lie.

They say, every one, another lie. The American Communists speak about religious liberty in Russia, but are disowned by their Russian comrades.

In his testimony, Rev. Wurmbrand also described the fate of the religious leaders of Rumania after the Communists took power.

He had been imprisoned with clergymen of the Catholic, Protestant, and Jewish faiths. "With us," he testified, "nearly all the Catholic bishops have been killed under tortures. Two or three, perhaps, have escaped." "In Rumania I have been in prison with Jewish rabbis. I could give their names." The Communists, he said, "make no distinction in persecuting religion."

In bringing charges against clergymen, Rev. Wurmbrand said that the actual crime is the instruction of children and youth about Christ, although the Communists "rarely say this."

At times, he said, clergymen are charged with theft. The amount of the Sunday collection must be reported to the government, and pastors must get permission to use any of the money. If any money is used for church purposes without government sanction, the pastor is branded a thief.

Charitable work is forbidden, and the sale of Bibles is considered illicit commerce.

Catholic priests, he said, are often accused of sexual offenses if "girls come to confess to them. Lies are said, and they are put in prison. Others are accused of currency offenses or counterrevolutionary activity."

In its May 2, 1967, issue, *Look* magazine quoted Roger Garaudy, French Communist Party theoretician:

We [Communists] are told, "You offer your hand when you are not in power and your fist when you are in power." At the beginning, Marxism arrived in countries where Christianity was reactionary and was battled against as a political party and not as a religion. This fear of persecution has been spread by elements that are political and not religious.

When asked to comment on the Garaudy statement, Rev. Wurmbrand replied that—

the Communists don't bring any political accusation against those whom they have put in prison.

They say they have spread only religion. They don't accuse this Mrs. Sitsh that she had said any counterrevolutionary words to her child. She has taught him the Gospel.

So they say they put men in prison for exclusively religious motives. * * *

He then added:

I have been in a prison with the Communist leader of Rumania, Patrashcanu, who brought communism to power in Rumania. He has been in the same cell with me and has been so tortured until he became mad. And then he was shot.

Ana Pauker, Vasile Luca, and other Communist leaders have been in the same prison with me.

They have put in prison those who brought them to power. I would suggest to Mr. Gus Hall and to Mr. Aptheker and to other American Communists, they should go to a church and pray to God, in whom they don't believe, that communism should never come to power in America, because as long as they have capitalism in America, they are free.

If communism comes to power, they are shot. In Russia, in Rumania, in Bulgaria, the Communists have killed the Communist leaders.

On the subject of "dialogue," Rev. Wurmbrand suggested that we should ask Roger Garaudy and Herbert Aptheker to—

go first to Moscow, to Peking, to Bucharest and dialogue with your own comrades and say that they should release all the Christian prisoners and that they should give the children back to their parents.

The dialogue, he said, "is a lie." To a statement by Archpriest Borovoi of Russia that his country was an example of "happy collaboration" between the Communist revolution and Christians, Rev. Wurmbrand replied:

We gave our backs, and they gave the whips. We gave our liberties, and they gave the jails. We gave our children, and they had the joy to bring them up in the atheistic manner. We gave our necks, and they gave the bullets for them. That has been the collaboration.

Rev. Wurmbrand also provided the committee with translations of two "doctrinal statements" on religion emanating from the Soviet Union in 1967:

The fight against religious remnants is * * * an inseparable part of the entire ideological activity of the party organization. The party orients all its organization and its ideological institutions towards aggressive, atheistic activity. (*Pravda*, January 12, 1967.)

The second statement, published in the *Communist of the Armed Forces*, February 1967, declared:

Religion and scientific communism can have nothing in common nor be related to each other, as was proved by scholars of Marxism-Leninism. In the future all the forms of religion will be thrown on the rubbish heap of history.

THE NEW COMMUNIST PROPAGANDA LINE ON RELIGION

THURSDAY, AUGUST 10, 1967

United States House of Representatives,
Subcommittee of the
Committee on Un-American Activities,
Washington, D.C.

PUBLIC HEARING

A subcommittee of the Committee on Un-American Activities met, pursuant to call, at 10:20 a.m. in Room 429, Cannon House Office Building, Washington, D.C., Hon. William M. Tuck (chairman of the subcommittee) presiding.

(Subcommittee members: Representatives William M. Tuck, of Virginia, chairman; Edwin E. Willis, of Louisiana, chairman of the full committee; John C. Culver, of Iowa; Richard L. Roudebush, of Indiana; and Albert W. Watson, of South Carolina.)

Subcommittee members present: Representatives Tuck, Willis, and Roudebush.

Committee members also present: Representatives John M. Ashbrook, of Ohio, and Del Clawson, of California.

Staff members present: Francis J. McNamara, director; Chester D. Smith, general counsel; and Alfred M. Nittle, counsel.

Mr. Tuck. The committee will please come to order.

We have a quorum present. This subcommittee of the House Committee on Un-American Activities is convened this morning to hold hearings pursuant to a resolution adopted by the full committee on March 8, 1967. The resolution adopted on that date reads as follows:

BE IT RESOLVED, That hearings by the Committee on Un-American Activities or a subcommittee thereof, be held in Washington, D.C., or at such other place or places as the Chairman may determine, on such date or dates as the Chairman may designate, relating to the extent and character of Communist propaganda and conspiratorial techniques employed within the United States to promote the objectives of the Communist Party in the United States and to advance the purposes of the world Communist movement by the dissemination of false and misleading information concerning Communist doctrine and practices in regard to religion and ethnic and minority groups, the legislative purpose being to provide factual information to aid the Congress in the enactment of any necessary remedial legislation pursuant to the mandate to the Committee by House Resolution 7 of January 10, 1967, and Public Law 601 of the 79th Congress.

Sixty-two years ago, Lenin wrote:

"Religion is the opium of the people." Religion is a kind of spiritual vodka in which the slaves of capital drown their human shape and their claims to any decent human life.

Forty years ago, Stalin wrote:

The [Communist] Party cannot be neutral towards religion. . . . Anti-religious propaganda is a means by which the complete liquidation of the reactionary clergy must be brought about.

In 1946 an official Soviet organ, *Young Bolshevik*, stated:

Dialectical materialism, the philosophy of Marxism-Leninism and the theoretical foundation of the Communist Party, is incompatible with religion. . . . the [Communist] Party . . . is bound to oppose religion.

Going back to Lenin again, he stated in 1909 that "Marxism is . . . relentlessly hostile to religion."

Earl Browder, for many years the leader of the Communist Party in this country, stated that "the Communist Party is the enemy of religion."

We are all too familiar with the many facts produced from the time of the Bolshevik revolution until a few years ago which demonstrated that, when Lenin, Stalin, and Browder made the above-quoted statements, they were unquestionably speaking the truth in regard to the Communist Party. Brutal suppression and persecution of all religions has been a trademark of communism everywhere.

As recently as 1964, angered and frustrated by its failure to destroy religion in the U.S.S.R. after 45 years' effort, the Soviet Communist Party established an Institute of Scientific Atheism to direct an intensified campaign against religious beliefs at every level and in every walk of life in the Soviet Union.

But now the Communists are speaking a different language. The leading theoretician of the French Communist Party, Roger Garaudy, was in the United States recently to deliver a series of lectures, including several on campuses of church-affiliated educational institutions. Basically, his message was that there must be "dialogue" between Christians and Communists, that they can learn from one another and work together to their mutual benefit.

Early this year, in a midwestern city, the president of a university chapter of the Communist youth group, the W.E.B. DuBois Clubs, told a group of Christian clergymen that, while "Marxists are still atheists," Marxists and Christians can—and should—work together. He urged his clergymen audience to reject the traditional Christian doctrine of "turning the other cheek" and instead to "hate their oppressors and fight them," to the end. He claimed that the Marxist attitude toward religion had softened.

Are this young man and the French Communist theoretician deviationists who have turned away from, and broken with, the official doctrine of communism as it is enunciated by Moscow?

The answer is "no." They are propagandists of the new Communist line on religion, a line promulgated by the Kremlin and now being widely disseminated in the non-Communist world.

The July 1966 issue of *Political Affairs*, an official monthly organ of the Communist Party, U.S.A., was devoted completely to the subject of "Communism and Religion." It featured eight articles on the subject, five of them written by key leaders of the U.S. Communist Party, including party boss, Gus Hall, and Herbert Aptheker, the party's leading theoretician.

The basic message of this special issue of the Communist organ was that communism and religion are no longer incompatible, that Christians and Communists can work together, and that they should do so.

At the 1966 convention of the Communist Party, a young Communist leader, a former seminarian, stated that there is "no contradiction between being a Communist and a communicant."

The new draft program of the Communist Party, U.S.A., published in 1966, claims that the party's membership is composed of both believers and atheists; that Communists see many values in religion; and that in a Communist United States "full freedom of conscience and worship will be guaranteed."

These recent statements by Communist officials and publications, if sincere, are certainly earth-shaking. If they are genuine, they reflect a major and fundamental change in basic Communist doctrine, a change that could have far-reaching effects in all parts of the world, a change that could reshape the thinking of millions of people on the subject of communism.

The Communists, of course, have made many false and treacherous statements in the past to serve their devious purposes. The 50-year history of their dealings with non-Communists on all levels, governmental and otherwise, is filled with examples of this—calculated, cynically and grossly false statements made by Communists and their agents for no other reason than to mislead non-Communists about the real nature and intent of communism.

Is the new Communist line on religion another example of this, or does it actually indicate a real change in communism?

It is the purpose of this hearing to develop for the record facts that will help Congress and the American people answer this question.

I now offer for inclusion in the record the order of appointment of the subcommittee to conduct these hearings:

AUGUST 9, 1967.

To: Mr. FRANCIS J. MCNAMARA,
Director, Committee on Un-American Activities.

Pursuant to the provisions of the law and the Rules of this Committee, I hereby appoint a subcommittee of the Committee on Un-American Activities, consisting of Honorable William M. Tuck, as Chairman, and myself, Honorable John C. Culver, Honorable Richard L. Roudebush and Honorable Albert W. Watson, as associate members, to conduct hearings in Washington, D.C., commencing on or about Thursday, August 10, 1967, and/or at such other times thereafter and places as said subcommittee shall determine, as contemplated by the resolution adopted by the Committee on the 8th day of March, 1967, authorizing hearings concerning the extent and character of Communist propaganda and conspiratorial techniques employed within the United States to promote the objectives of the Communist Party and world Communism by the dissemination of false and misleading information concerning Communist doctrine and practices in regard to religion, and other matters under investigation by the Committee.

Please make this action a matter of Committee record.

If any member indicates his inability to serve, please notify me.

Given under my hand this 9th day of August, 1967.

/s/ Edwin E. Willis
EDWIN E. WILLIS,
Chairman, Committee on Un-American Activities.

Are we ready to call the witness?

Mr. SMITH. Yes, sir.

Mr. TUCK. Will you stand and raise your right hand?

Reverend Wurmbrand, do you solemnly swear the testimony you are about to give to this committee will be the truth, the whole truth, and nothing but the truth, so help you God?

Mr. WURMBRAND. Yes, sir.

TESTIMONY OF REV. RICHARD WURMBRAND

Mr. Tuck. Proceed.

Mr. Smith. Reverend Wurmbrand, will you give the committee your full name, please?

Mr. Wurmbrand. My name is Richard Wurmbrand.

Mr. Smith. Where and when were you born?

Mr. Wurmbrand. I was born on the 24th of March 1909, in Bucharest, Rumania.

Mr. Smith. Are you a citizen of the United States?

Mr. Wurmbrand. No; I am a Rumanian citizen.

Mr. Smith. What is your present status?

Mr. Wurmbrand. I am here as an alien resident.

Mr. Smith. When did you come to the United States and from what country?

Mr. Wurmbrand. I came the first time in April 1966 from Rumania through Norway.

Mr. Smith. How did you happen to come to the United States?

Mr. Wurmbrand. I was bought out from Rumania. I was ransomed from Rumania by church organizations. I came to Norway, and there I was invited to preach with the American Lutheran Church and in a meeting of the NATO staff.

I told them what is happening in Rumania. Especially at the NATO meeting there was an interesting happening. A colonel of the American Army asked me: "What do you think about peaceful coexistence with communism?"

I have been so many years with pickpockets in prison, I have learned something from them. In a minute his purse was in my pocket, and then I stretched my hand to him and said:

"Let us peacefully coexist, but your purse will remain in my pocket.

"That is what the Communists wish. They have taken half of Europe. They have taken China, they have taken Rumania. They have taken Russia itself by force.

"Never has any nation chosen in free elections the Communists as their rulers. They have stolen a third of the world, and now they say 'Let us peacefully coexist.' They should give back what they have stolen."

Those of the American Lutheran Church and the military chapel in Oslo were so much impressed by what I preached that they immediately collected money to send me to America, to tell you the same things.

I will here express my thankfulness to Pastor Myrus Knutson of Our Savior's American Lutheran Church in Los Angeles and to Colonel Sturdy, a military chaplain, who have helped with this, as well as to the anonymous contributors.

Mr. Smith. Under what circumstances or, in other words, how were you able to leave Rumania?

Mr. Wurmbrand. I have been in Rumania in prison 14 years. I was sentenced to 25 years, but in '64 a general amnesty has been given.

At that time a delegation of our Rumanian Government was in America asking for loans and for trade. It was somehow whispered in their ears that the administration of America is under the pressure of public opinion and that the public opinion in the West does not like it that there are so many in prison.

Next day we were driven out of prison. So much can America do for the enslaved peoples.

Then I resumed my Christian underground work. But very soon they began to rearrest those whom they had liberated. I was under such danger, and then church organizations paid for me a ransom of $7,000—the Norwegian Israel's Mission and the Hebrew-Christian Alliance. And I express here my thankfulness to them, too.

Mr. SMITH. Were the authorities not afraid to let you out of Rumania?

Mr. WURMBRAND. Well, that is a very interesting question. They have let out from Rumania several of those who have been in prison. And we have asked ourselves why they do it.

On one side, they believe very much in brainwashing, and they are not wrong in believing this.

I don't wish to use names here, but there are in America Rumanian clergymen who have been in prison with me, who have been tortured just like me. And some of them are praising communism here, under the influence of the brainwashings in prison.

There have been all kind of threats, so they believe that it is dangerous to speak out.

But there is also another motive. A Catholic priest, when the passport has been handed to him to go to Western Germany, asked the secret police: "But don't you fear to send me out to Germany? You have kept me in prison 7 years. I have passed through so many horrors. I will tell them there."

And they answered laughingly: "You just tell them! Tell them everything! Tell them the worst things! The more you will say, the less you will be believed. Nobody will believe you."

Americans did not believe about the gas chambers and the furnaces of Hitler until the American troops did see them; so it happens with the Communist atrocities. They seem incredible.

I myself, during the nights, ask myself sometimes if everything has not been a nightmare. So incredible are the Communist horrors.

The Communists threaten former prisoners, but they don't fear much that we will speak out.

Mr. SMITH. What is your profession?

Mr. WURMBRAND. I am a Lutheran pastor.

Mr. SMITH. And where are you employed?

Mr. WURMBRAND. Now I am employed by a mission called Mission to Europe's Millions. It is an American branch of a British organization called European Christian Mission, a mission which has as its program the spreading of the gospel in Europe.

I am the representative for the missionary work in the Communist world.

Mr. SMITH. Where is the headquarters of this mission?

Mr. WURMBRAND. There is one in London and one in Glendale, California.

Mr. SMITH. Is it supported by interdenominational groups?

Mr. WURMBRAND. Yes, Christians of all kinds of denominations and individual churches are supporting us.

I formerly belonged to the organization "Underground Evangelism," which I left for earnest motives.

Mr. SMITH. Do you have any credentials which would identify you?

Mr. WURMBRAND. Yes; but first I wish to add a few words about the purpose of this mission, if I may. The purpose is to help the underground church behind the Iron Curtain: to support its pastors, to support families of Christian martyrs, to supply them with Bibles and with other Christian literature.

Mr. SMITH. Do you have any credentials that would identify you in your activities?

Mr. WURMBRAND. Yes.

As coming out from Rumania, we could take not a bit of paper with us, I have asked many people who have known me in Rumania to give me credentials.

Here I have one of a member of our royal family: "I can positively answer that Wurmbrand is genuine. I knew about him since 1947 * * * . He made a deep impression upon me. What he relates coincides with what I know. I am glad that you are taking a positive interest in this man because he is really worth it. * * *"

One from Peter Dinisiu, Baptist preacher of Rumanian origin. He says: "I have known Rev. R. Wurmbrand since the year 1936. He was head of the Swedish Israel's mission, and representative of the World Council of Churches, one of the best known Lutheran pastors of Rumania."

Here is a credential—I can't give the name—of one of the biggest Christian leaders of Rumania. It has been smuggled out from Rumania:

"I recommend Mr. Wurmbrand as one of the most faithful of Jesus Christ."

Alexander Balc, Baptist pastor in Akron, Ohio, also of Rumanian origin: "I know Wurmbrand personally from Rumania. He is one of the best known Lutheran evangelic pastors. He was head of the Swedish Israel's mission and representative of the World Council of Churches. He is generally known in Rumania as fighter against Communism." Myrus Knutson, from Our Savior's American Lutheran congregation in Los Angeles: "His life and story have been thoroughly checked. He is trustworthy and responsible."

The Norwegian Israel's mission: "He has passed 14 years in prison."

The Friends of Israel Missionary Society, Philadelphia: "We know Wurmbrand * * *. The valuable services he has rendered to his congregation in time of need and his total dedication to the cause of Christ have made Richard Wurmbrand one of the most outstanding Protestant pastors and Christians of our day."

Mr. Robert Tobias, formerly assistant director in the World Council of Churches in Geneva: "Mr. Wurmbrand was liaison representative for our work of the World Council and Church World Service."

The head of the Luthern World Federation in Israel, Magne Solheim, formerly in Rumania, speaks also about my work in the World Council of Churches and 14 years of prison. I quote: "In the period of 1946–48, when I also served as representative of the Reconstruction Department of the WCC in Rumania, Rev. Wurmbrand worked together with me, doing a very precious work."

Here is a very interesting credential from a pastor of Rumanian origin, Milan Haimavici, who has passed himself 7 years in Communist prisons, and how he tells the story of his and my torture: "Since I was put many questions concerning Pastor Wurmbrand, and was also tortured, I know how he was tortured.

"The tortures consisted in hour-long beatings on the whole body and at the bottom of the feet, in long hunger, in being kept for weeks in places where you could only stand, in eating out of pots where we were compelled to fulfill our necessities * * *"—I myself have eaten of such a pot—"* * * in being put barefoot on burning coals.

"Before God I can swear that I passed through all these tortures, and like me, many other thousands of prisoners, and Pastor Wurmbrand, too."

Peter Trutza, Baptist professor at the Northern Baptist Theological Seminary, of Rumanian origin, says the same about my representing the World Council and my being known as Lutheran pastor and fighter against communism.

Priest Galdau of the Rumanian Orthodox Church in New York: "He is a Lutheran pastor well known for his struggle against communism while in Rumania. He is the author of several books on this subject.

"He represented, together with Pastor Magne Solheim the World Council of Churches in Rumania."

The International Christian Hebrew Alliance: "He has been ransomed from Rumania by the payment of a large sum of money, and our organization had a large part in raising the funds from Christian people for this ransom."

Pastor Göte Hedenquist, Swede, former secretary of the World Council of Churches, speaks also about my 14 years of prison and my work for this institution.

I could give some 50 other credentials, but I think these are enough. I wish to make it clear that by presenting these credentials, the persons mentioned are not implied in responsibility for what I say. I speak only in my own name, as a private person. Neither these persons, nor my mission, have been consulted nor have any responsibility for what I will say. I specify also that, although I worked for the WCC, I don't agree at all with its friendly attitude towards Communists.

Mr. TUCK. Do you wish, Mr. Smith, to file those documents as exhibits with the record?

Mr. SMITH. I do not believe, Mr. Chairman, that it is necessary to include these documents in the hearing record. I would suggest, however, that they be retained in committee files.

Mr. WURMBRAND. The documents are at your disposal. You can have photo copies of them.

The CHAIRMAN. Mr. Wurmbrand, you are of German extraction?

Mr. WURMBRAND. No, I am a Jew.

The CHAIRMAN. Let me ask you: Is there as much persecution of the Jews as there is of the Christians behind the Iron Curtain?

Mr. WURMBRAND. In Rumania I have been in prison with Jewish rabbis. I could give their names—Schoenfeld, Deutsch Junior, and many others. I don't remember all the names.

The Communists make no distinction in persecuting religion.

As about Russia, Svetlana Stalina says that her husband, only because he was a Jew, for no other reason, has been deported for 11 years. She says that her sister-in-law, also only because she was Jewish, has been deported and since killed in a concentration camp.

Well, more and more, these facts must be known.

The CHAIRMAN. It must be known, and I am so grateful to you that you, who are of Jewish extraction, are bringing them out. I appreciate it.

Mr. WURMBRAND. Very often the anti-Communists are smeared as being anti-Semite. Sorrily, it is sometimes true, but more often not. In any case, this is one argument which cannot be brought against me, because I am Semite and love my Jewish people.

The CHAIRMAN. That is right.

Mr. WURMBRAND. Usually it is said that Stalin has been anti-Semite.

Now, Stalin has never killed a Jew. He has had henchmen, and these henchmen had the names of Mikoyan, of Khrushchev, Kosygin, of Brezhnev. They were with him in the central committee when this whole anti-Semitic politics has been practiced. It is madness that some Jews in America and other parts of the world are ready to die for this anti-Semitic communism. Some of them—surely very few, but some of them.

Djilas, an old Communist, who has been put in prison by Tito, says in his book about the anti-Semitism which reigns at the Kremlin, and about which he himself was afraid.

A Christian can only love the Jews. From the human side, Christianity is Jewish.

Horrible things are happening with the Jews in Russia from a religious point of view. In Kiev there are something like 300,000 Jews who have only one synagogue, with one rabbi 80 years old.

In Vilnus there is also only one synagogue.

The chief rabbi of Georgia has been hanged with the head down.

In Tashkent there has been recently a pogrom. Jews have been driven to suicide in Russia, being called to the secret police and asked to organize anti-Israel meetings.

Now, they could not organize them, first of all because Israel is right, and then they belong to Israel. And they were driven to suicide, because otherwise they would have gone to prison.

Last week in Poland, officers of Jewish background have been dismissed from the army.

The attitude of the Communists towards the Jews has been seen in the recent Middle East crisis, when they were entirely on the side of the enemies of the Jews.

I am very sorry that there are still some Jews—I believe there are not many—who don't realize that to be a Communist means to be a traitor to your Jewish race.

The CHAIRMAN. That is what concerns me so much. I am glad to have that for the record and to have you clarify that point.

Mr. WURMBRAND. Marx has been an anti-Semite. Marx himself has been of Jewish origin, but he has written a fierce anti-Semitic book called *The Jewish Question*. I would recommend Mr. Aptheker, the theoretician of the American Communist Party, to read it.

The official attitude of the Communist International towards the Jewish question is fixed in a book of Heller, an official book of the Communist International, and it is called—it was first published in Germany—*Der Untergang des Judentums (The End of Judaism)*. In it they say that communism means the end of Judaism.

I hope that Mr. Aptheker, for whom I have sentiments of love, as for every man, may not have read this book. I would recommend him to read it and to read *The Jewish Question*, written by Marx.

Communism has been anti-Semitic from its beginning.

My knowledge is that not a lot of Jews are Communists. The Jewish Communists are very few, but noisy, giving thus the wrong impression that they are many.

Mr. SMITH. Reverend Wurmbrand, have you been known by any other name or names?

Mr. WURMBRAND. Oh, yes, I have had in my life very many names, out of two motives.

First of all, I worked in the underground church. Also, in Rumania I led the secret Christian missionary work in the Soviet Army.

Our country was invaded by some 1 million Russians. I speak Russian fluently, as good as English, you may say as bad as English. But in any case, I speak it. I organized immediately the secret work among them and, also, the underground work among Rumanians. And where I went, in every village and in every town, I had to have another name.

Now only I understand parts of Scripture as I have never understood before. I never understood before why in the *New Testament* it is written: Simon called Peter, Jacob and John called the sons of the Thunder, Simeon called Niger, John called Mark, and so on.

Now I understand. The first Christian church was a secret organization. And we also operate in the Christian work in Communist countries with secret names. We never introduce ourselves.

I have published books under all kinds of pseudonyms.

And then, when I was put in prison, I was told the first day: "You are henceforth Vasile Georgescu. You are not allowed to say to anybody your real name."

I have not been arrested in a formal manner. I have been kidnaped from the street. That was their manner of arresting at that time.

There have been protests against my arrest. The Swedish Ambassador and others protested. The Communists answered that I have not been arrested, that I have disappeared. Therefore, that a guard after a glass of wine may not say the secret that I am in prison, the guard had not the right to know my right name.

The same, Greek Catholic bishops, and other prisoners known abroad were kept in prison under false names.

Mr. SMITH. Why was that necessary?

Mr. WURMBRAND. Having nicknames in the underground church was necessary, because we were dogged by the secret police. If in a village, in a town, it would have been known that Wurmbrand has arrived, I would have gone to prison immediately. But with false names I could hide myself. As regards the other name, the secret name given to me in prison, that was their manner to hide from people that these and these people are arrested.

The people were kidnaped from the streets. They disappeared. They answered to my family when she inquired: "Oh, who knows? He may have found a girl somewhere and have disappeared," and things like this.

The Swedish Ambassador, Patrick von Reuterswärde, was told by Ana Pauker, who was at that time head of our Department of State, that "Wurmbrand is not arrested. He is somewhere, fled from the country."

Therefore, they kept us under a false name.

Mr. ASHBROOK. Could I ask a question at this point?

Reverend Wurmbrand, you stated that the arresting authorities, on occasion, would keep your real name or the real name of other religious prisoners secret, in effect, from the public.

Is this because in Rumania there still would be a resentment to the state having an oppressive doctrine against religion? They are afraid to meet public opinion?

Mr. WURMBRAND. I will answer you simply. I preached in Kansas City, and there I was introduced with the words: "Here is a pastor from a Communist country."

I protested: "I am not from a Communist country. I am from a Christian country. I am from a Christian country oppressed by the Communists."

Practically nearly nobody is Communist with us. The Communists are a small, an infinitesimal minority, which rules by terror and by deceit, which was imposed upon us by the Russians. Rumania is not a Communist country.

I have been 14 years with thieves and murderers, and not with gentlemen, I may have lost manners and may be impolite. But I have sworn here to say the whole truth, and I will say simply what I know and what I think.

My son is studying now in a Californian university. On the walls it is written, "American murderers." That is not written in our universities. If anybody would write it in a Rumanian university, the Rumanian students would tear it down.

In our country nobody can burn an American flag. He would be trodden under the feet of the Rumanians.

We are not a Communist country.

Mr. ASHBROOK. Then it would be fair to say that it would not be generally known, for example, among Christians in Rumania that you were in prision for 14 years.

Mr. WURMBRAND. They feared that it would create an agitation. In the end it was known, but they wished to delay the agitation as much as possible.

Mr. ASHBROOK. Thank you.

Mr. SMITH. Mr. Wurmbrand, will you give us your address here in the United States?

Mr. WURMBRAND. I am very gladly at your disposal to give the address privately to the committee, but I can't give it in public.

Mr. SMITH. Is there any reason for that?

Mr. WURMBRAND. Yes; because I am under the menace of being kidnaped or killed.

Mr. SMITH. I see.

Mr. WURMBRAND. Before leaving Rumania, I was called twice to the secret police, and I was told: "Now you leave [Rumania]. Preach Christ as much as you like, but don't touch us! If you touch us, for a thousand dollars we can find a gangster who will finish you * * *"— which was not true, because they can find him for $500—"* * * or we can bring you back."

(I have been myself in the same cell with a Rumanian Orthodox bishop, Vasile Leul, who has been kidnaped from Austria and has been brought back in Rumanian prisons, and many others like him.)

"Or we can destroy you morally. We can find out a story with a girl or money or so, and people will believe it. So be very careful about what you do!"

I have very earnest motives to be careful about giving in public my address, the more so as I know recent cases of very bad things which have happened to others.

Czeckoslovakian agents of the Communist secret police with the names of Jaroslav Kovar, Jindrich Zelenka, and Josef Ruzicka have killed 11 men and 2 women, living in Western Germany, Switzerland, and other countries of the free world because, for some motive, their lives were considered as dangerous to the Communists.

I give you the names of some of those killed:

Christa Wanninger, killed in Rome; Marcel Leopold, killed with a poisonous arrow; Dr. Paul Stauffer, killed with five bullets.

Matus Cernak received a parcel in Munich. When he opened it, it exploded and killed three persons.

A defector from the Czech Communist police disclosed the names of the murderers and all the circumstances.

The brother of our Prime Minister disappeared. What wonderful conditions there are in our country, you can see by the fact that the brother of our Prime Minister, Ceaushescu, defected, something like 2 months ago. He went to France. He was not accepted by Germany, because Germany wishes to make trade with Rumania and money is always more important than the souls of men. He went to France, and from France he disappeared. Now he is in a Rumanian prison. I could give you many such cases which have happened. Therefore, I can't give in public my address, but I can give a post office box. My address is P.O. Box 11, Glendale, California 91209. The Communist kidnapers may seek me at the post office box!

Mr. ROUDEBUSH. Mr. Counsel, I would like to ask a question.

Reverend, can you give me or the committee any cases that you know of, of former religious leaders from behind the Iron Curtain who have been kidnaped or killed in this country?

Mr. WURMBRAND. In this country, I don't know.

Mr. ROUDEBUSH. You do not know of any?

Mr. WURMBRAND. I don't know in this country; no.

Mr. ROUDEBUSH. Another question I would like to ask you. You said that when the secret police turned you loose they had no fear of what you had to say, because they felt that you would not be believed by people of the free world.

Mr. WURMBRAND. Yes.

Mr. ROUDEBUSH. Have you found this phenomenon to be true?

Mr. WURMBRAND. Well, partially, it is true. I preach nearly every evening in some auditorium or in some church of all kinds of denominations. I have preached with the Catholics and with the Lutherans and with the Jews and with everybody. The rank and file believe us, weep when they hear what is happening there, only they have no influence at all.

When you arrive to the top leaders of churches, some either disbelieve you or ask you, beg you, not to speak.

I was asked by one, I don't wish to tell his name——

Mr. ROUDEBUSH. You mean the heads of churches where you appear ask you not to be candid about your experiences?

Mr. WURMBRAND. Yes, surely.

Mr. ROUDEBUSH. This is an amazing thing.

Mr. WURMBRAND. I publish next week a book of mine called *Wurmbrand's Letters*, my letters to the leaders of the World Council of Churches and Christian bodies of America, also to Catholic leaders.

I have been asked, "Well, speak about Christ! We know that you are a very gifted preacher and we will help you in this. You can say everything," and so on. "But don't speak"—I was told these very words: "Don't speak against communism, because this will make men hate the Communists and the Russians."

I answered, "I am a man who comes not from a jungle, but from a subterranean prison of a jungle. I am a man who has nearly never seen a book 14 years. I have nearly never had a pencil in my hand 14 years.

"You give me this advice, but I know about you personally that you marched against injustice done to the Negroes in the South. Now I am a foreigner here and I don't know if these injustices are real or alleged. Suppose that they are real. You marched against them. Did you not fear that you will make the Negroes to hate the white?

"Why is it that in any town of America you can see movie pictures about the atrocities of the Nazis against the Jews—and such movie pictures should exist. It has been a huge crime to kill millions of Jews. My family has been killed. But I can't agree that only Jews should not be killed. Russians shouldn't be killed either, nor Rumanians or Chinese, and Communists are killing these everywhere. Show me one motion picture in all America about these atrocities which I will document from the Soviet press, about these atrocities happening today."

And I was told, "Don't speak out about these things."

Then I asked them, "How is it possible? Please explain it to me. How is it possible that you gave me exactly the same advice as the Communist secret police gave me? They also told me, 'Preach Christ and don't speak about communism.' "

The rank-and-file Christians and Jews simply feel that I tell them the truth, and they respond and they weep.

But the Communists are not concerned about them, because they know that these don't decide things. As to the top leaders—not all, but many of them—and I don't know how to measure my words, but they were not on our side.

I came as a naive to America. I believed if I was told that this is a head of the World Council or the National Council or of the Presbyterian Church or of the Lutheran Church, I believed that he is a representative of Christ on earth, and I went to him as to a brother. I didn't find with them the sympathy of Christ for the martyred church.

I can't really speak about what is happening in the Communist camp. I am only a man. When you sleep—I can't sleep, because I hear what is happening there. When I go to a church, you hear there the songs. I hear the cries of the tortured martyrs. There exists another Christian song, which is sung in the Communist countries. "Ah, ah, ah, don't beat! Don't beat!" This is a Christian song which I have heard 14 years day and night. I hear it even now, the song sung there. There is with me an emotional involvement. And I think that every Christian must feel like me. We Christians are one body. And even if you are not a Christian, you are a man and you must feel with another man. I would feel with a Muslim. I feel with a Communist, if he is tortured. I feel with a criminal. A criminal should not be tortured.

I have been in Philadelphia. The newspapers announced a public rally against Vietnam. I have never seen a public rally against the government of our country. Such a thing does not exist in the Communist camp.

So I went out of curiosity and I stood near the pulpit. A Presbyterian pastor led the rally. As long as he spoke against Johnson and against the war it was not my business. I am a foreigner. I will never mix in internal American affairs. But then he began to praise communism. This, I could not bear. And as he was a small man and I am tall, I made just like this [gesturing], and he was no more on the pulpit. I was on the pulpit. And I said to him, "How do you dare to praise the Communists? The Communists are torturing Christians." He asked: "What do you know about communism?"

When he asked me, "What do you know about communism?" I said, "I am a doctor of communism and I will show you my diploma as a doctor." With this, I undressed myself to the belt. I showed him. I have 18 marks in my body. I did not know that it is illegal in your country to undress yourself in a public place. I said, showing the scars: "This the Communists have done to me."

So one asked me, "Why did they do you this?" I said, "Because I am a murderer. Do you think that murderers should be tortured? Has Oswald been tortured? Has Ruby been tortured?" And I asked the audience, "Do you think that murderers should be tortured?" The audience said "No."

"Well," I said, "I have never been charged with murder. I am a clergyman, just like he is, and this is a Judas. He praises the Communists instead of Jesus."

And then his adherents booed him as a Judas. One cut the wire of the microphone, and the police took me out.

The CHAIRMAN. Reverend, I am not suggesting what I am about to say is directed against your testimony, but you are saying things that are hard to believe here.

Mr. WURMBRAND. Yes. I know it myself. Incredible things happen. There are some American clergymen who praise communism.

The CHAIRMAN. I can't conceive of responsible, religious people not wanting you to speak out against communism and cautioning you to keep your mouth shut. To me that is incredible.

Mr. WURMBRAND. Well, if you will allow me, I will show you the documents, exclusively of the Soviet press, not mine, in which they say about sentencing Christians. If I can read these newspapers, everyone in America can read them and can have them translated.

They say about taking away children from their parents because their parents have told them about Christ. How would you like that your children should be taken away? Here is what the Soviet press says. I will present to you all these documents.

They say about confiscating Bibles. They say about all the horrors which they commit. I went with such documents to Christian leaders, but some of them were busy with something else: to picket before the White House against the war in Vietnam.

I don't speak out here for or against the war. I don't wish to mix in this thing, but why did they not picket before the Russian Embassy for their Christian brethren who are persecuted?

I will present to you the documents. You will see the documents exist. And if some church leader has been misinformed before, he has the information from me now, and I am ready to appear to debate with leaders of your Communist Party, with leaders of your church organizations, who say that there is a religious liberty there. They should contradict my documents.

They can contradict me, but not the documents.

Socrates said, "I can be contradicted. Truth can't be contradicted." With Socrates you finish very easily as being a homosexual, but with his philosophy, you can't finish like this. With me, you can finish. I am a sinner. But what about the documents I present?

One has written to me a letter: "I know a sin of yours from 1930." He may have heard it from a Rumanian. There was a threat in these words and a hope that I will be quiet in the future.

My answer is: In 1930, I had the age of 20, and I was not a Christian. I can send you a list of 50 sins which I have committed in 1930, and of another 50 sins which I commit today. Don't you believe in the remission of sins by the blood of Jesus? How can a Christian leader remind a sin since long washed away in baptism?

I am a sinner—I know it myself; no one has to remind me—but the facts which I present about Communist persecution of religion can't be contradicted. These facts must be known by the church members, by America, by the whole free world. We are oppressed there. We are tyrannized. I bring you the cry of those oppressed. If you will allow me, I will show you one document.

Mr. SMITH. Mr. Chairman, Reverend Wurmbrand some months ago forwarded some 50 documents to the committee we expected to introduce with his testimony today. These documents are in the Russian language. At the request of the committee, the Library of Congress prepared English translations of the documents. However, Reverend Wurmbrand has brought with him documents more up to date than those previously forwarded, which he will introduce with his testimony.

Since the committee has not had time to secure Engl'sh translation of the documents, he will summarize the contents of each as he introduces it.

Permiss on is requested that all these documents, both those previously forwarded as well as those he will introduce today, be received and be made a part of the record with determination to be made later as to whether they will be reproduced as exhibits.[1]

The CHAIRMAN. Well, I can understand that these documents emanating from Russia, or wherever, saying those things, I can understand the accuracy of those, but I still say it is incredible to me that a responsible churchman or responsible man in America would try to stifle your talking against communism.

Mr. WURMBRAND. The word "church" is an ambiguous word. There exists a church, the bride of Christ. I have seen her dying for Christ and loving Him. And there exists an institutional church in which you become a leader because you have some academic qualifications, and not because you have burning love towards Christ, a church in which there exists no tears for those who suffer, no joy for Christian victories.

The real church, it weeps with us and it jubilates with us. And now if I may present, I have chosen on'y——

Mr. TUCK. Unless there is objection to the procedure suggested by counsel, and the Chair hears none, you may proceed.

Mr. SMITH. Reverend Wurmbrand, you heard the opening statement of the chairman in which he pointed out that the Communist

---

[1] The exhibits submitted by Mr. Wurmbrand are retained in committee files.

Party of the United Státes, in a reversal of its old longstanding propaganda line of the incompatibility of communism and religion, is now claiming that Christianity and communism are compatible; that Christians should work with Communists and can do so to their benefit.

Quoting from Herbert Aptheker's item, which he wrote in the *Political Affairs* magazine of July 1966—this magazine is an official organ of the Communist Party of the United States——

Mr. WURMBRAND. I know it.

Mr. SMITH. —and Herbert Aptheker is the recognized theoretician of the Communist Party of the United States. Quoting, "Marxism, of course, opposes religious persecution; it opposes coercive methods aimed at religion."

I also quote from a writer, Miss Betty Gannett, a high Communist Party, U.S.A., functionary and present editor of *Political Affairs* writing on the subject of "Religion in the USSR" in the same July 1966 issue of *Political Affairs*. Quoting: "Contrary to prevalent misconceptions in our country the Soviet Union has at no time passed laws to restrict freedom of conscience or the right to religious worship. On the other hand, it has not only proclaimed but *guaranteed* religious liberty by law." And that "no organ of Soviet power conducted antireligious propaganda * * *."

Do you have any documents with you today which bear on this as to whether these claims are true or false?

Mr. WURMBRAND. I have, first of all, the doctrinal statements of our Communists. Here, in America, they state what you have read.

When the Communists came to power in Rumania they were very weak and played also the role of being friends of religion. We had a Communist Party only of 10,000 members when they arrived to rule. They have been imposed by the Russians. Vishinsky came to our King and beat a fist on the table and said, "You must nominate this government." Now, being so weak, the Communists have convened in Rumania in the building of the Parliament, a congress of cults. There were 4,000 priests, pastors, rabbis, mullahs, of all kinds of religions. The Prime Minister of the Communist government, Petru Groza, delivered a speech and said, "Oh, yes, in olden times in Russia there have been bad things about religion. These have passed away since long. You should be on our side." That was in '45. "You should be on our side. We will support religion." And the Minister of Interior Affairs, Teohari Georgescu, an old Communist, made big crosses and kissed the icons. We have seen that. And priests believed them; 4,000 priests and pastors cheered the Communist Prime Minister. There was only one pastor out of the 4,000 who protested there on the spot. One pastor out of 4,000. This one went to prison. You have him before you today.

Everywhere the Communists, until they have the power, say that they are the friends of religion.

Now I will show you what they do after they come to power. I have here hundreds of documents. I will not show them all. I have chosen only those of '67 and the latest days of '66, but I have also about '65 and '64, and before.

First of all, two doctrinal statements. On the 12th of January '67, in the *Pravda*. That was a few days before Podgorny saw the Pope:

In true accord with Leninist traditions our party is continuously giving great attention to the problems of atheism. The fight against religious remn ants is not in the nature of a campaign of an isolated or self-sufficient event. Rather, it is an inseparable part of the entire ideological activity of the party organization. The party orients all its organization and its ideological institutions towards aggressive, atheistic activity.

The party journal, *Communist of the Armed Forces*, from February '67, writes:

Religion and scientific communism can have nothing in common nor be related to each other, as was proved by scholars of Marxism-Leninism. In the future all the forms of religion will be thrown on the rubbish heap of history.

"All forms of religion," also this form of religion which collaborates with communism.

This is the doctrinal statements. Now I will give you the cases of sentencing of Christians. Here is the newspaper. I will submit it to you.

Bakinsky Rabotshii (Worker of Baku), a Russian Communist newspaper of the 20th of February '67, an article called, "The Fanatics Should Not Put Hands On Children." They describe in it a demonstrative trial in Mir Bashir. A demonstrative trial is not held in a courtroom, but in a great auditorium. They compel hundreds of workers from all factories and students to attend. You must be there. You must boo the accused ones. The accused one in this case is Vassily Romanov of Armenian origin. His crime, the newspaper says, is that he has won many children and youths for Christ. He preached about the Last Judgment and the approaching coming of Christ. His worst crime is that he said, "We must love our enemies." That is a crime.

My son studied in a Communist school. Do you know how in the elementary classes he was taught arithmetic? "If from 22 Americans you have shot 18, how many remain?" Therefore, they have to oppose the teaching of love to our enemies.

Romanov has been judged according to article 141 of the Criminal Code of the Soviet Republic of Azerbaijan, an article which exists in '67. And the American Communists say there exists no law to forbid to a man religion, to forbid to a man to speak about Christ.

You will see immediately other articles.

This Romanov has shown to children the religious films which were smuggled in. The missionary organization to which I belong works also at bringing in secretly religious films in Communist countries. Romanov has taught children to become soulwinners and to spread in school religious poems written by hand.

Then the article says, "We are patient towards religious sects, as long as they do not touch our youth." They don't mind an old woman of 70 to believe.

The newspaper saith further that the Adventist children don't wish to attend school on Saturday. Children win each other for Christ, and the pupil Alexander Zhukov, under the influence of Christianity, refused to carry the Red flag.

Our youth does not carry the Red flag, knowing that it is stained in the blood of Christians. That is how our youth reacts.

I can't express admiration enough for our youth. With us in a school the professor told that man is from the ape. Then he asks the pupils, "What do you think about it?" Up stood a young girl and said, "Comrade Professor, I am thankful for what you have taught us today. I always wondered how it is that the Communists are so bad. Now you have explained it to me. They are from the apes."

Pravda Vostoka (Truth of the East), another Communist paper, of the 22d October '66. The title of the article is, "You Are Not Judged For Your Faith, Hrapov."

No, he is not judged for his faith. In the beginning of the article the reporter says, "I have spoken with the accused one. He said that he suffers for his faith. It is not so." And now the reporter says why Hrapov suffers. Hrapov, Bohn, Hartfeld, a Jew, and others were members in Tashkent of an unofficial Baptist church. These are the Baptists who don't wish to compromise with communism. They gave out a secret religious magazine called *The Herald of Salvation*. Now these accused ones are charged that they have spread the following criminal sentences in this magazine. "The resurrected God wishes to free us all of the slavery of dependence upon the world." "Every friendship of the world is spiritual prostitution."

Hrapov organized the Brotherly Fellowship of Christian Youth, something like your YMCA. He had secret a printing press for Christian literature. And the children under his influence refused to wear the red neckties. That is what the Soviet press saith on the 22d of October 1966.

I present to you the pictures. From *Pravda Ukrainy* of the 4 October '66. It is the picture of one of the greatest heroes of the Christian faith in Russia, Prokofiev. He has been already thrice in prison for running secret Sunday schools for children. He was released. He resumed his activity. And now together with others he is before court again.

Sovetskaya Rossiya of the 23d of August 1966. "Put a Stop To This." That is the title of the article. They describe a trial in Rostov-on-Don. The accused ones are charged that they organized a religious demonstration on the streets on the 2d of May '66, and that at that date, they baptized 40 boys and girls. What a horror. To baptize boys and girls! They had also a secret printing press.

The Communist newspaper says, "Lays on the conscience of the accused ones the organization of Sunday school for children in which children aged 8 and 11 were taught the word of God. They are judged on basis of article 142 of the Criminal Code of the Russian Republic."

Now whom should I believe? Mr. Aptheker or the Russian press? Who knows communism better? The Communist Party of America says that there exist no laws against religion in the Soviet Union, and I have given you already proofs about sentences on the basis of article 141. Now we have article 142. "The six were sentenced to different terms," says the newspaper. It doesn't say what terms. It may be 20 years.

They have baptized 40 boys and girls, among them a student in medicine, a student in engineering, members of the Communist Youth. The Communist paper says that the witnesses of the defense who were called before court, "had a fanatic attitude."

In the secret literature spread to the youth, they called to active propaganda of religious conceptions, and they said, "Take in your hands the spiritual sword, the word of God."

They say the Baptist books are dangerous. One phrase which is incriminated is "Take children to burials, that they may see that it has no sense to be busy with vain things."

I must say, I have been converted to Christianity by going through cemeteries. I asked myself once I will be dead. Snow will fall upon my grave. Here I have political and all kinds of other ideals and I wish to have money and I wish to have girls, and everything will finish once with a corpse in a tomb. Then I saw a party which can give eternal life. I have found the party of Christ.

Well, these are the crimes for which you are put in prison in Russia. The leader of the underground church is an engineer. We have in it Russian intellectuality, we have students, engineers. They teach children to read the Bible. But afterwards these children tear down their red neckties.

The Herald of Salvation, which must have a very large circulation, although it is illegal, teaches mothers to give antidotes against materialism. Under the influence of this magazine a child says, "The atheists are our enemies." The Communists say that the spirit of religious education is antisocial.

Here is another newspaper. *Pravda Ukrainy* of the 12th July '66. The title of the article is, "They Received As They Deserved." Again a demonstrative trial in the town of Nikolayev against Zaitshenko, Maria Yakimenko, and others. The names of these martyrs should be on the lips of all Christians here. We know about St. Therese and St. Basil and St. Martin of hundreds of years ago, and the martyrs of today are never mentioned.

I said to one of the biggest American church leaders, "Here I have in my pocket the list of 150 Protestant pastors who have recently been deported to Siberia. Not all have arrived. Some have died under tortures." He didn't ask for the list. When I asked him, "But don't you wish to have them on your prayer list? How is it that you don't ask me for this list? What are you doing?" he still didn't ask me for this list.

Those last mentioned by me were sentenced to 5 years of prison. They were Pentecostals.

Pravda Ukrainy, of the 4th October '66. There is an article called "The Law Is Written For Everyone." Tried in Kiev, Bundarenko, Velitchko, Overtshuk, and others on the basis of article 138 of the Code of the Ukrainian Republic. So every republic has an article against religion in their law. They have many republics.

The accused ones are charged to have said: "Submitting itself to human regulations, the church loses God's blessings." "The official leadership of the Baptist Church submits itself to the Communists." "In our days, Satan dictates and the church accepts all kinds of decisions which contradict the commandment of God." They forbade the atheistic burial of a Christian child. They said the youth must gather around Christ. They got 2 to 3 years' prison with severe regime.

The last sentence of the article in the newspaper is, "In our country, nobody is judged for his religious convictions. But nobody has a right to contravene the Soviet law."

That is their line. They say that this Hrapov and others have done nothing else than to spread the religion. Oh, religion is free, but you are not allowed to break the law. And the law says that you are not allowed to spread religion.

If they can lie like this in an article in Russia, the lies of the Communists in America are very little indeed.

Sovetskaya Rossiya of the 22d of November '66. Trial against three ladies, also for have taught children. Children even fled from home and attended Sunday schools. And the children said to their mothers, "If you don't allow me to go there, I will leave home."

I myself have had in Rumania a beautiful case of a young girl who attended our secret Sunday schools. Then her parents forbade it. She said, "If you forbid me, I will not eat anymore." And three days she hungered. Then the parents, afraid, said, "Go, but eat." It was their only daughter. She said, "No, I will not go until you come with me," and she brought the parents, too, to Christ.

In the Communist camp, the children fight for Christ. The Communists boast in this article that they have put in prison these three ladies.

In America, church leaders have contested even that an underground church exists.

Now here is an underground leaflet printed in the secret printing press in Russia [showing leaflet]. In Russia there exists secret printing presses, secret Sunday schools, so there exists surely an underground church. I asked myself, "If such a powerful underground church exists about which the Soviet press writes, and there are a hundred other articles about it—I don't wish to take your time—why is the underground church not represented in the World Council of Churches? Why is the underground church never invited to send representatives here in America? Metropolitan Nikolai comes and others. They should be welcome. I love every man. But why are the heroes of the underground church never invited? And even when one member of this church came, some of your American church leaders wish him to be silent. As for me, I have not been silent in Communist prisons and I will not be silent here.

These are the facts about sentencing Christians. I have published a book, *Today's Martyred Church, Tortured for Christ* with facts about persecution taken from the Soviet press. And in my second book, *Wurmbrand's Letters* there will be other facts taken from the same source. Anyone can write to me at Post Office Box 11, Glendale, California 91209, and I will keep him informed about the facts. Then there will be no doubts more.

Mr. TUCK. We will take a 5-minute recess.

(Members present at time of recess: Representatives Tuck, Willis, and Roudebush, of the subcommittee and also Representatives Ashbrook and Clawson.)

(A brief recess was taken.)

(Members present at reconvening: Representatives Tuck and Roudebush, of the subcommittee, and also Representative Clawson.)

Mr. TUCK. The committee will please come to order.

You may proceed.

Mr. SMITH. You may proceed with your presentation, Mr. Wurmbrand.

Mr. WURMBRAND. Now, these facts about sentencing of Christians, I think, would be enough. If anybody wishes to know how the arrested Christians are treated, I would tell them to come to me, and I will show them my body.

Christ when he was not believed by St. Thomas simply undressed himself. I don't boast about the scars which I have. They are not mine; they are signs of the torturing of my fatherland and of my church.

The Communist camp gives martyrs every year. Hmarof Kulunda has been only 3 months in prison. His corpse has been given back to his family. He had burnings, at hands and feet. The lower part of the belly was split, and he had bruises over his whole body.

Here I show you the picture of the prison of Kazan, where many Christian prisoners are kept. And here is the island of Novaya Zemlya.

I often wondered how it is that poor Russia can compete with America in making missiles and rockets. I could not compete with Rockefeller; how can they compete?

Very simply, they work with slave labor. To an engineer, you have to pay $20,000 or $30,000. They would arrest him. Then he works without wages. He is beaten and tortured. And in the island Novaya Zemlya, Christian prisoners are working on rockets and missiles.

This is the picture of Marshal Warenzoff, who was at the head of the slave labor for producing missiles.

I spoke about prison, and to be in prison is bad, but there comes a much bigger tragedy than being put in prison. I will show you what the Soviet press says about children taken away from their parents. I know what this has meant for me.

Believe me, that in winter, I pressed my bare breast to the icy iron bars to quench the fire of longing after my child. I know what it means, not to see your children during years.

And now, I have here *Znamya Yunosti*, a Moscow newspaper, of the 29th March '67. They tell the case of Mrs. Antonina Ivanovna Sitsh. The court in Kaliningrad deprived her of parental rights and took away her son Vsetsheslav because she told this son to witness for Christ in school, and, as often as atheistic movie pictures were shown, to keep his eyes closed, not to look at this dirt, something which I would recommend also to American children, when sometimes dirt is shown at the TV.

For his Christian attitude, Vsetsheslav was taken away from his mother. Now, the newspaper says that this Mrs. Sitsh committed a second crime. Not only that she taught her children Christianity, but she has stolen her child from the atheistic boarding school and has sent him to the town of Vitebsk, to brethren in faith.

But there he was discovered, because in school again he witnessed for Christ. He was taken back. With the complicity of somebody of the staff of the atheistic boarding school, the mother smuggled in to him a notebook with Bible verses in miniature.

And now her second child, Leonid, at the age of 8, knowing that the brother has been taken away from mummie, has also said to his teacher: "I pity you. You will go to hell because you don't believe." And he tore down the red star from the wall.

Here is the tragical case of Kolya Sviridov. That is a child of the age of 9. At this age he showed already an exceptional religiosity. As it appears from the article, he seems to be of the old royal family of Russia.

Because of his exceptional religiosity, he was taken away from his mother, but in the atheistic boarding school, he continued to pray, so they have given him in the hands of Captain Hutorin of the Communist secret police. A child of 9 in the hands of such a brute!

The officer of the Communist secret police determined the child to say, "There are no gods." But *Komsomolskaya Pravda* of the 22d of May '66 is not sure what the child meant, because the child has been told about mythology, that there existed gods of gold and of marble. Perhaps he meant them. He didn't say that he does not believe in God.

When his mother was allowed to see him, he asked: "Who is this woman?" He didn't know any more.

Imagine what this child has passed through! At the age of 9, he has already myocarditis. And here in America, the lie is spread that there is religious liberty in the Soviet camp.

This picture is from *Doshkol'noye Vospitaniye* of March 1966. The secret police has entered in a house and has siezed four children in the attitude of prayer. They publish it. The children will be taken away from their mothers.

Here is a picture of the trial of Makrinkova. Six children have been taken away from her. Who can imagine what suffering this means?

I have known mothers from whom their children have been taken away. In a house which has been full with the noise, with the laughter, with the kicking of children, now there is a great silence of God.

I have seen these mothers; they were like bits of stone. You could not speak with them.

Six children taken away, and that is called "religious liberty," even by some Western church leaders.

Here is *Ogonyok*, a Moscow magazine. Lazarev has run a secret Sunday school in this little hut pictured here [showing picture]. For this, he has to respond.

I could give you many such facts. I have chosen just a few about depriving parents of parental rights.

Here about the Bible: "The Bible is a poison." It is not allowed. Here is *Trud*, a Moscow newspaper, of the 6th of July 1966. They give the picture of hundreds of confiscated Bibles. They say it always: "We will not allow our people to be poisoned." In this article, they accuse Mr. Murray, who is one of the directors of the British European Christian Mission and of the American Mission to Europe's Millions, to which I belong, too.

They accused him truthfully that he tried to bring these Bibles into Russia.

Here is a handwritten Bible in Lithuanian. They write it by hand. They have no printed ones. [Shows pictures.]

There exists in Moscow a Catholic Church. De Gaulle has been there. He goes to many places. In this church he could have read this catechism. [Shows catechism.] The catechism is mimeographed. They have no printed catechism in the church of Moscow.

Here is another story from *Ogonyok*, the Russian magazine, the story of a Mrs. Persis, put in prison because secretly she has produced candles and icons.

Now, I myself am Protestant. We don't use icons, but I consider it is a crime to put somebody in prison because he believes in an icon and makes an icon. In Russia, for this he is put in prison. That is the "religious liberty" as proved from the Soviet press.

Now, in matters of communism, who knows communism better? *Pravda*, Kosygin, or Mr. Aptheker, the theoretician of the American Communist Party? Who of these should I believe? Aptheker should go to Mr. Kosygin, and they should convene what they should say.

It is said that witnesses were brought against Jesus at the trial, but what one witness said did not correspond with the other witness. I would recommend to the Communists, when they wish to lie, they should come together and convene how to lie.

They say, every one, another lie. The American Communists speak about religious liberty in Russia, but are disowned by their Russian comrades.

Now about closing of churches. My own church in Bucharest is a theater now. My church, the Rumanian Lutheran Church in Bucharest, the former building of the British Church Mission, is a theater. Only a pastor can know—you love your church as you love a child—what this means.

But that is an assertion of mine. Now the proofs.

Sovetskaya Moldavia of the 13th of August 1966! I speak now with a little bit of national pride. You know what Moldavia is. That is a part of Rumania which the Russians have stolen from us, our Bessarabia.

This is one of the parts of the Soviet Union where the underground church is the most powerful. They could take away our province; they could not eradicate the religion. Here is the article entitled "Where the Bells Rang."

The article is of 13 August 1966. They say about closing the churches in Nikolayev, in the province of Orhei and the church of Floreshti, in the village of Cretzoaia and others. They have made of some of these churches dispensaries; of others, schools; of others, dancing clubs. They say it.

Here are pictures of different churches which are now museums.

That is the Church of the Robe of the Virgin Mary. That is the Cathedral of the Annunciation—a museum. That is also another picture of this same cathedral. [Shows pictures.]

Here is the new church at Klaipeda, completed in 1960. The steeple has been torn down, and the church is used as a concert hall. The Vilna cathedral is now an art gallery. And here we have a picture of a concert in this art gallery.

The Jesuit church and monastery at Kaunas is now a warehouse. And if you wish to see churches that are open—please see a Lutheran Church, if you like it. It is with grass as a roof. [Shows picture.]

And they say, "We have churches." Here you can see it. Who likes to worship in such a church?

Mr. TUCK. File these.

Mr. WURMBRAND. Yes, they will all be in.

Mr. ROUDEBUSH. Reverend Wurmbrand, you did mention some churches being opened. You mentioned the Catholic parish where General de Gaulle worshiped in Leningrad, I believe.

Mr. WURMBRAND. He was at a church.

Mr. ROUDEBUSH. Do you know of any bona fide church leaders, outside of those in the underground church, in the Communist world? Do you know of any sincere religious leaders outside of the underground?

Mr. WURMBRAND. Yes. I myself am a Protestant, but I love truth more as Protestantism. I must pay my homage, first of all, to Cardinal Wyszynski of Poland. He has been in prison and he continues to oppose communism.

There exist such official church leaders, too. There are some of the Eastern German Lutheran bishops who are in this situation, the same isolated cases of Rumanian official Baptist pastors. But, as a general rule, the leadership of the churches is entirely controlled by the Communists, and I will give you immediately the proofs of this.

Mr. ROUDEBUSH. But this is not 100 percent true? There are some genuine leaders?

Mr. WURMBRAND. There are some; yes.

Mr. ROUDEBUSH. Who are dedicated to Christ?

Mr. WURMBRAND. Yes, exceptionally. As a rule, it is otherwise. When you tell me in America that a man is a pastor of the Lutheran Church, then I know that he has made a seminary. You must not specify it to me. Otherwise, he couldn't be a pastor.

If you tell me that somebody is an official pastor in a Rumanian or a Russian church, I know that he is an informer of the Communist authorities. Without this, you can't be.

On Sunday you preach. On Monday you can be called to the so-called representative of the Government Council for the Affairs of the Religious Cults, and you are obliged to answer the questions: "Who has been in your church?" They don't care about those old ones. "What youth has been in church?" "Who is a soulwinner?" If they have confessed something, "What they have confessed?" "Who is zealous in prayer?" "What are their political attitudes?"

You have to say all this.

Now, there are some who try to say the minimum possible and to mislead the Communist authorities. There are such ones. There are some who say what happens, and there are some who have the passion to say more than happens. It has become a passion with them.

So in this sense, there is a difference.

The underground church is also infiltrated by the Communist secret police, but we infiltrate the Communist secret police, too.

Members of the underground church become officers of the secret police. Members of the underground church become leaders in the official church and tell us what happens there. These are very sincere Christians.

Now I have presented to you the facts about what is happening in the Communist camp.

Now, who are the official church leaders?

Karev is the general secretary of the Russian Baptists. He publishes in *Soviet Life* of June 1963: "The Baptist parents have the right to raise their children in the spirit of faith."

Now, should I believe Karev? Or should I believe this, what the Soviet newspapers say, that children are taken away from their parents if these give them religious education?

The Orthodox Metropolitan Pimen called Svetlana Stalina a Judas Iscariot, because she defected. These church leaders are stooges of the Communists.

M. Orlov, second chairman of the All-Union Council of the Union of Evangelical Christian Baptists, has said:

"The Evangelical Christian Baptists as well as all other Christians of the Soviet Union are thankful and praise God that the Soviet Government during the course of the past 40 years has acted according to the high ideals precious to Christianity, for these are also the ideals inherent in the Gospel."

So, the Soviet Government acted according to the high ideals of Christianity when it stole the Baltic countries, half of Poland, Bessarabia. It acted according to the high ideals of Christianity when it invaded Hungary. It acted according to the Gospel when, under Stalin, it killed millions of innocent men. The Baptist Orlov subscribes to all the horrors of all these years.

Another declaration of this so-called Baptist leader: "We deeply respect our Soviet Government, which has given us religious freedom and protects it from any violation whatever. In our country all churches and religions enjoy an equal and complete freedom."

These would be the main facts about Russia which I had to give you. If you wish, I can continue during hours, but——

Mr. SMITH. I think that will be enough. We will accept the rest of them for the record.

Mr. TUCK. We will accept the rest of them as exhibits into the record.

Mr. WURMBRAND. I have presented many other documents, sir.

Mr. SMITH. Reverend Wurmbrand, Roger Garaudy, the theoretician of the Communist Party of France, is quoted in *Look* magazine of May 2, 1967, at page 36, as having made this statement during his lectures in the United States on the dialogue between Christians and Communists:

"We [Communists] are told, 'You offer your hand when you are not in power and your fist when you are in power.' At the beginning, Marxism arrived in countries where Christianity was reactionary and was battled against as a political party and not as a religion. This fear of persecution has been spread by elements that are political and not religious."

Based on your experience, what comment could you make about this statement?

Mr. WURMBRAND. First of all, in the articles which I have presented to you, the Communists don't bring any political accusation against those whom they have put in prison.

They say they have spread only religion. They don't accuse this Mrs. Sitsh that she had said any counterrevolutionary words to her child. She has taught him the Gospel.

So they say they put men in prison for exclusively religious motives. But even if what Mr. Garaudy saith would be true, he gains nothing. It is a crime also to persecute somebody for political motives.

They put in prison not only counterrevolutionaries, but Communists, too.

I have been in a prison with the Communist leader of Rumania, Patrashcanu, who brought communism to power in Rumania. He has been in the same cell with me and has been so tortured until he became mad. And then he was shot.

Ana Pauker, Vasile Luca, and other Communist leaders have been in the same prison with me.

They have put in prison those who brought them to power. I would suggest to Mr. Gus Hall and to Mr. Aptheker and to other American Communists, they should go to a church and pray to God, in whom they don't believe, that communism should never come to power in America, because as long as they have capitalism in America, they are free.

If communism comes to power, they are shot. In Russia, in Rumania, in Bulgaria, the Communists have killed the Communist leaders.

In Bulgaria, Kostov has been hanged. In Hungary, Rajk has been hanged.

With us, Ana Pauker has been put in prison. Trotsky, Zinoviev, and so on, they kill each other.

It is a religion of hate.

Now, about this question of dialogue. I myself am all for a dialogue. First of all, the Communists should go to the other world and have a dialogue with the bishops and Christians whom they have killed. That would be a very interesting dialogue.

With us, nearly all the Catholic bishops have been killed under tortures. Two or three, perhaps, have escaped.

Bishop Aftenie died in an asylum for the insane. I have known him before. He was not insane. He has become insane under tortures.

Bishop Durkowitz, I have known him myself, also. Catholics said about him that the touching of his garment healed. This man has been killed in prison.

So they should go to heaven and have a dialogue there with those whom they have killed and continue to kill now, Protestants and Catholics and Orthodox.

In Red China, thousands of Christians are killed now. The Red Guards, who frog-marched diplomats on the street, where everybody sees, have cut, in Chinese jails, the ears and tongues and the legs of Christian prisoners, if they did not deny Christ.

One about whom it is said that he has passed through this ordeal is a renowned Chinese Evangelical Christian, the writer, Watchman Nee, and they should go and have a dialogue with him. That would be the right kind of dialogue.

If somebody attacks you, you have to fight. If the microbe attacks me, I have to fight against it.

Do the Communists accept this peace?

Here is *Kazakstanskaia Pravda* of the 4th of March 1967. The title of the article is "The School of the Irreconcilables." Under this title, they describe the Institute of Scientific Atheism, in Alma-Ata, where they are taught "never reconciliation, never peace with Christianity."

Now, you can't make peace only onesided. The gangster is against me with a rifle, and I am for peace. But if he doesn't put his rifle down, then I have to fight against him, and to do something.

Some people say: "We will not fight." But the Communists, from their side, fight.

Here I have the index of all works which have appeared in Moscow against religion. January '67, so many books against religion. February '67, other books against religion. March '67, April '67, May '67. And from *Semia I Shkola* of January '67: "All the clergy is illiterate and dishonest." This, they say in Russia.

And here they say to the clergy: "Please come and discuss with us, and we will be good friends."

I can't understand how this happens. I don't know how you will think about it. But when Suharto came to power in Indonesia, many hundreds of thousands of Communists have been killed.

I have publicly protested in the press against this. I said: "I have suffered under the Communists, but I can't admit that an unjudged man should be killed, whatever he has done. A rebel can't be killed before he is judged." I protested against this.

And now there are Christians who know that their brethren in faith are martyrized. They can have all these documents. I am a poor man and I could afford to have these translations. They can also have translators to translate all these things.

They can know them and they should be on the side of their brethren. And they should say to Mr. Garaudy and to Aptheker and to the other Communists: "You wish a dialogue? You go first to Moscow, to Peking, to Bucharest and dialogue with your own comrades and say that they should release all the Christian prisoners and that they should give the children back to their parents."

Kosygin has asked here that Israel should give back Jerusalem to the Arabs. I have read in the Bible that the whole of Jerusalem belongs to Israel. He says that the Israelians should give back the conquered territories.

Why does he not give some up? He has taken Lithuania, Latvia, Bessarabia, Hungary. Why does he not give them back? And why does he not give back the children that they have taken away to their parents?

It is a lie, this dialogue. And because there is an increase of interest in this dialogue, I wish to say that at a session of the World Council of Churches in Geneva, Archpriest Borovoi of Russia said these very words, that Russia is an example of "happy collaboration" between the Communist revolution and Christians.

Then I wrote to a leader of the World Council of Churches and said: "I can subscribe to what Borovoi has said. We collaborated very happily. We gave our backs, and they gave the whips. We gave our liberties, and they gave the jails. We gave our children, and they had the joy to bring them up in the atheistic manner. We gave our necks, and they gave the bullets for them. That has been the collaboration."

In this whole World Council of Churches, there has not been one man to slap this Borovoi.

At the Council in Nicaea, when Arius said that Jesus is not God, St. Nikolai stood up and slapped him for saying this. And the legend of the Orthodox says that the Virgin Mary appeared and put on him his bishop's garments, proving there are certain cases where you can't react otherwise.

Nobody booed Borovoi.

And when Archbishop Nikodim said that there is full religious liberty in Russia, although his comrades from the Soviet press say that it is not true, one of the biggest American church leaders went and kissed him.

Now what should I say about these things? I must say that I suffer in America more than I have suffered in Communist prisons.

In Communist prisons I was with Jesus. I forgot that communism existed. When a child has died, after a year or two the scar closes somehow, and you are no more so sad. But when you see a child dying, then it is horrible.

Rumania, its independence has died already. But here in America, I see this infiltration, this spreading of lies, youths believing them. And I have wept more tears since I am in your rich America than I have wept in 14 years of prison.

I was in the house of an American millionaire. I had never seen an American millionaire, how he looks like. I find that he looks just like any other man.

He invited me in his home. It was a beautiful home. I, who have never had in my life a bicycle, was now in a rich home and had coconut pie before me.

I began to weep. He asked me: "Why do you weep?" I said: "Because of your children! They are playing there with toys on the carpet. I had a vision for a moment that they will be beaten at the bottom of the feet, as I have been beaten at the bottom of the feet, if you will not defend yourself against this horrible lie of communism."

I have given you facts. And again I call leaders of the Communist Party and leaders of churches who say that there is a religious liberty there; they should come and contradict these, my documents. They should come before television, wherever they like. I will come to debate, and they should prove that these documents are not true. They can't be contradicted.

(At this point Mr. Clawson left the hearing room.)

Mr. SMITH. Reverend Wurmbrand, the new draft program of the Communist Party, U.S.A., published in 1966, makes the following statement: "Full freedom of conscience and worship will be guaranteed in a socialist United States."

Do you have any factual knowledge bearing on the truth or falsity of this statement?

Mr. WURMBRAND. First of all, wherever the Communists were in opposition, they have always said this.

Lenin had taken the defense of the Protestant sectarians in Russia, until he came to power.

In Rumania, they have done also this.

Now, if they have done this everywhere and then, when they came to power, they oppressed the Christians, this does not mean that the American Communists will also do this. But we wish from them a proof of sincerity.

Are they against the persecution? And the clergymen who sustain that in Russia there is liberty, are they sincerely against the persecution?

Then I would propose to them something. I have seen once men picketing before the White House. I went there and I introduced myself. I told them my story, and I said:

"If you have something against Johnson, I am not for him and I am not against him—I have nothing to do with your American politics. You picket him as much as you like. But you are clergymen, and you are Christians. Come and picket with me the Soviet Embassy."

They should prove. They should give the proof that they are against religious persecution, taking an attitude against the Soviet Government, against the Chinese Government, against the Rumanian Government.

And they should say: "We are against you. We are your enemies, because you persecute the Christians, and we have declared here publicly that we love the Christians and wish dialogue and friendship with them. Those who persecute our friends are not our comrades. Out with you!"

If they will say this to Kosygin and the rest, then I will believe them, that really there has been a change of position.

If not, I can't see sense in their statements.

Mr. SMITH. Do you know of any persons recently arrested in Rumania because of their religious faith?

Mr. WURMBRAND. Oh, yes, I can give you the names: Ghelbegeanu, Alexandru, Gabrielescu, Balautza, Janos, Irina, Istvan, and many others.

Mr. SMITH. What were the charges?

Mr. WURMBRAND. The last ones were arrested some 2 months ago.

Mr. SMITH. Are these people in prison?

Mr. WURMBRAND. Yes, many of them are in prison now. We don't know exactly the number. But it is considered that something like 200 Greek Catholic priests are in prison. The same for many of other religions.

Mr. SMITH. What was the nature of the charges brought against them?

Mr. WURMBRAND. There is a difference between Rumania and Russia. In Russia the Communists usually acknowledge that it is for religious motives. With us, they very rarely say this. The real motive is teaching of children and youths about Christ.

But the charges brought before court are sometimes "theft," which consists in the following.

With us the finances of the church are under the control of the state. If there has been a church offering, you, the pastor, have to report to the government that on this Sunday the offering has been so much.

It goes to the national bank, and you as the pastor are allowed to use this money only with the approval of the Communist authorities.

Now, these approve only a minimal salary for pastors. My salary when I left Rumania was $28 a month. I think it is not very much— $28 a month!

They don't permit any charitable work. In Russia and Rumania there exists not one private philanthropic organization. Imagine a government which forbids a philanthropic organization. I and you and he, we are not allowed to give everyone $10 and to care for some children or for some old men. You are not allowed to use the offerings for church repairs, and so on.

So some pastors have said that church funds belong to the church and, without asking the Communist government, they have used this money for church purposes. For this they are considered as "thieves."

Others are in prison for speculation. Only the government is allowed to make commerce, but the government doesn't sell Bibles, doesn't sell prayer books, doesn't sell such things. So a priest has to sell them, or a pastor.

If he has sold, they say: "Oh, we don't put you in prison for religion, but you have broken the law against illicit commerce."

Against the Catholic priests, very often the accusation of sexual offenses is used if girls come to confess to them. Lies are said, and they are put in prison. Others are accused of currency offenses or counterrevolutionary activity.

Mr. SMITH. Reverend Wurmbrand, you mentioned a while ago the fact that there was an underground church in Rumania——

Mr. WURMBRAND. Yes.

Mr. SMITH.—and in Russia. Would you care to comment a little further on that and tell us how they worship, how they conduct their services?

Mr. WURMBRAND. About the underground church in Russia, I have given you many facts.

In Rumania there are three major organizations of the underground church. There exists an Orthodox underground. We are in very good relationship with each other. There exists an Orthodox underground, "Oastea Domnului," which means in English "The Army of the Lord." It is something like your Salvation Army. It is considered a forbidden secret organization.

The Communists say that it has 300,000 adult members. When they announced a secret meeting, 6,000 farmers came to a secret meeting. You can't arrest 6,000.

The police came, arrested just a few leaders. When the leaders were judged before court, my wife was there. Farmers from the whole country surrounded the court. And when the prisoners were brought in, they began to cry: "We have committed the same crime. We believe like them. Arrest us, too."

You can't arrest a whole country. With us, nobody is on the side of the Communists. Men are rather on the side of Christ.

We have a second, a Baptist underground. They are called The Awakened.

There exists a Presbyterian underground. They are called Bethanists, something like your Christian Endeavor here. They have passed and pass through prisons.

One of the leaders of the Bethanists has been sentenced to many years of prison for the following crime.

He preached on a Sunday about a Bible verse, in St. John 21 in which Jesus says: "Throw your nets on the right side."

The next day there was a secret police officer, who said: "How did you dare to say that nets should be thrown on the right side, on the side of imperialists, and not on the left side?" The pastor went to prison.

Here many Unitarian pastors are of the left wing. With us, Unitarian pastors are in prison. A Unitarian pastor, a friend of mine, was put in prison because he preached on a Christmas Eve that when Jesus was a little child, Herod wished to kill Him, but His holy mother fled with him to Egypt and there he was concealed.

The pastor was brought before the court and told: "You meant us. You wished to say that we, the Communists, like Herod, killed the Christians and that you hope in the end, Nasser will pass to your side. Therefore, you mentioned Egypt."

Notwithstanding all this terror in the Communist camp, now being often in your cathedrals, I long for the beauties of the underground church behind the Iron Curtain.

When we meet sometimes in a wood, the vault of heaven is the vault of our cathedral. We are like the Catholics. We would not worship without incense. The smell of flowers is our incense. The chirping of birds is our organ. The shabby suit on a pastor who has recently been released from prison, shines on him like the robes of a priest. And when the evening comes, then angels are our acolytes and light, as candles, the stars of the skies. The underground church is beautiful.

Mr. SMITH. What is the attitude of Christians when arrested and brought before the courts in Russia and Rumania?

Mr. WURMBRAND. I will tell you a few facts.

First of all, again to my national pride, *Sovetskaya Moldavia*, reporting about the Rumanian province of Bessarabia, says that seven boys and three girls have been arrested for having publicly sung Christian hymns.

They were brought before the court and sentenced to 5 and 6 years of prison. When they received the sentence, they knelt down and said: "God, in Thy hands I surrender my spirit."

And the audience in court—the newspaper saith—began to sing the same hymn for which these ones have been arrested.

At another trial, a Christian prisoner has been asked by the judge: "Why do you continue to spread your faith, which is antiscientific?"

So he answered: "Do you know more science than Einstein? Einstein has given his name to the universe, and he believed in God and in religion, so that is enough for me."

A judge, again, bagatellized and mocked religion at a trial.

Five hundred Baptists had been arrested in Moscow for the demonstration on the 16th of May 1966, and when the judge mocked religion, then an accused one asked: "Mr. Judge, could you please explain to me the following thing?

"The manure of a cow is like a pancake. That of a horse is another form. That of a rabbit is like a little egg. Could you explain to me this difference in manure?"

The judge looked at him and said: "I don't know."

Then the accused said: "You know nothing about manure and you dare to mock about the Bible."

Mr. SMITH. Five hundred Baptists were arrested in Moscow, you mentioned. What year was that?

Mr. WURMBRAND. May '66.

Mr. SMITH. May 1966?

Mr. WURMBRAND. A secret leaflet has been smuggled out. Here is the secret leaflet in which the Russian Baptists tell what has happened. [Shows mimeographed leaflet.]

They have been beaten on the streets and put in prisons.

Another demonstration has been in Kiev and also in Rostov-on-Don.

Now the Communists will celebrate their 50th anniversary of the Communist revolution. They don't celebrate their victory. They celebrate our victory, because after 50 years the underground church has come overground. There are demonstrations on the streets, and children tear down the red neckties. They confess Christ in baptism.

We have won the battle, and not they. They have rubber truncheons. We have the truth. We have the love, and we have God.

Mr. SMITH. And I take it from what you say that the spirit of Christianity is still very much alive with the people, in spite of the oppression.

Mr. WURMBRAND. Oh, yes, or it could not be explained that in every town, the Communist newspapers speak about it.

Nobody cares about some little things. If it would not be a big thing, this growth of the underground church, they would not be so alarmed about it.

Mr. SMITH. How have the prison experiences of Christians affected them with respect to their religious faith?

Mr. WURMBRAND. I can say as well about myself as about other Christians that it has only strengthened our faith. I will give you just one example.

With us a minister has been arrested. His name was—let us say—Florescu. It is an imaginary name. I don't give the real name. Even under tortures, he did not betray the secrets of the underground church.

Then they brought his son, aged 14, stripped him naked, and began to beat him in the presence of the father. The father was a man. I wonder if I would have borne it.

I have been with this man in the same cell after years, and you could still see the horror on his face. And at a certain moment he could not take any more, and then he cried: "I must tell everything! Otherwise they will kill you!"

And the son said: "Father, don't do me the shame to have a parent a traitor, a Judas. Don't betray."

Then the Communists in furious rage beat him and tortured him worse. The father said: "Alexander, I must say everything. Otherwise you will die."

And the child answered: "Father, if I die, my last words will be 'Jesus and my fatherland.' I can die for them. But don't betray."

We are, as you know, a very backward country. We don't have your techniques. We have no burning of draft cards. We are too backward for this.

With us, who loves Jesus, loves fatherland, too, and dies for it. Cases like this, we have had many. The Christians have become like steel with us. The diamond is nothing else than coal under high pressure. The high pressure of communism has changed Christians into diamonds.

Mr. SMITH. Reverend Wurmbrand, in view of what you told us, is conscientious exemption from military service permitted in Russia?

Mr. WURMBRAND. Oh, no. In no Communist country.

Mr. SMITH. Your information concerning persecution of Christians and other religionists in Soviet Russia does not appear to accord with information brought back by tourists who have attended church services in Moscow and Leningrad. Would you care to say something about that?

Mr. WURMBRAND. What happens? If you go to Moscow, you find a packed Baptist church. And they come and they say, "What a beautiful service in this Baptist church." Thousands of American tourists have seen it, and I dare to assert that this Baptist church in Moscow does not exist. They have all had a hallucination. Moscow is a town with 7 million inhabitants. For 7 million inhabitants, there exists not a Baptist church. This church is not Baptist. It is Baptist, Methodist, Pentecostal, Mormons, Presbyterians, Adventist, all together. It is not Baptist. For all the Protestants of a town of 7 million inhabitants, there is one church.

Now why does this one church exist? I wonder that one church can dupe Americans. I have been in a congregation when a big preacher preached and showed slides of this church and explained the liberties there. I am not a very mannered man, so I stood up during the sermon and said, "Please show me the slide of the second Baptist church in Moscow." He surely could not. "Please show me the slide of the Sunday school for children in this one Baptist church! Please show me the youth meeting in this church! In every church of the world there exists a table in which you can buy a Bible or something like this. Please show me such a table at this church!"

Don't you see that it is a church for duping? The same, there exists one Catholic church. There exists a few Orthodox churches, and so on. These are just for duping. There is nothing earnest. The most real church is the underground church. The official church can't satisfy the religious necessities of the people.

I love the Russians very much and I feel very bad when people speak evil about the Russians. It is never the Russians, it is the Bolshevists who oppress the Russians. The Russians have remained fundamentally religious.

Mr. SMITH. Recently, a very famous minister in this country conducted a well-attended religious service in Yugoslavia. Does it not appear from this fact that religious freedom exists in Yugoslavia? What comment would you care to make on that?

Mr. WURMBRAND. It depends on what he preached. The Gospel has two sides. The one side is the proclamation of the Kingdom of God, and the other is the criticism of sin. Now Herod would not have beheaded John the Baptist because he said, "Repent, the Kingdom of Heaven is near." He beheaded him when he said, "You, Herod, are bad." Jesus was not crucified for the Sermon on the Mount. He was crucified because He said, "Woe unto you, hypocrite Pharisee." But there has not been one denunciation of communism by any American preacher who went to a Communist country. He may have said about Jesus the most beautiful things in the world. I have attended their sermons. No one of them has come to say, "Communism is a crime. You have committed the crime to kill millions of my brethren. I am on the side of the martyrs and against the oppressors, I am for religious liberty."

This they should have said, and, "I protest against the crime that you poison the children and the youths with atheism."

If he would have said this, after 5 minutes he would have been driven out of the country. That is one thing.

So I think that preachers who go there without saying this truth are not faithful to Christ. Christ, if he would go to Yugoslavia or Poland or Rumania or Russia, would say this, as he has said it in Jerusalem 2,000 years before. Rarely faithful American preachers also come. I can give you a name. An American, Dr. Starmer, the head of the Baptist mission in Italy, came to Bucharest. I was there. He has been formerly the head of the Baptist seminary in Bucharest, so he understood Rumanian. He could not speak it, but he understood everything. And now he came to preach. Translated for him a Rumanian Baptist who is known as an archtraitor, a stooge of the Communists. Starmer preached the truth and Popa translated what he liked. Starmer understood Rumanian and there was a public scene. He turned to his translator and protested. "I have not said this. You mistranslated." But he could do nothing else, and so it went on like a comedy. So it happens in all the Communist countries.

I contest that anybody can go to any Communist countries, even to Poland, which is the best one, and say the full Christian truth, which always includes the condemnation of communism, of its atheism, of its terror, and be free to preach and be translated correctly. A diluted Gospel, in which you say a few nice things, this you can preach.

Mr. SMITH. Before the Communists came to power in Rumania, were there any persons who foresaw and warned about what would happen to religion under the Communists?

Mr. WURMBRAND. Oh, yes; we have had great personalities. We had in the Orthodox Church Metropolitan Gurie, the metropolitan of Bessarabia, who was a very active anti-Communist fighter. He finished as many American anti-Communists finish. He was besmeared. He was a man who thought only about God and fatherland. And he was besmeared to have stolen. He had a huge administration with hundreds of employees and he passed his time in prayer and preaching instead of controlling books. So they finished with him simply. All Christians in Rumania knew him to be honest. I could tell you many such facts. Besmearing is one of the great weapons of communism. I wonder what they will say about me, but they will surely find out something to besmear me. They will find some tool of theirs in the church for this.

When I testified before the Senate, the next day the Rumanian Communist newspaper of America published about me, "Oh, Wurmbrand, what is he? He has a German name. So he surely has been in prison as a Nazi. And when he spoke about fatherland, he said it with a German accent 'Vaterland,' so he is a German and he has been in prison for nazism."

Then I wrote to them a letter and I said, "Please excuse me, but I am a Jew. So if I would have liked to be a Nazi, Hitler would not have accepted me, in any case." And the whole thing was finished. But they will find something else, that I am an adulterer, a thief, a traitor, a burglar, a murderer. Something they will find, and people will believe.

Mr. SMITH. Prior to the Communist rule of your country, do you have any information as to whether there was any Communist infiltration into Rumanian churches?

Mr. WURMBRAND. I am very thankful that you put this question, and I will give you facts. I have here in the audience several Rumanian friends and great personalities. I have here Dr. Brutus Coste, who would be perhaps Prime Minister of Rumania, if Rumania would be free, and he can confirm the facts quoted by me as well as my role in Rumania.

Professor Constantinescu Iashi was one of the best known theological professors of Rumania. When the Communists came to power, he became Communist Minister of Culture, a member of the Communist government. People opened their eyes and asked, "But how? You have prepared for ministry thousands of priests. How is it?" He answered, "I have been sent by the Communist Party in the theological seminary."

Bende, the secretary of the Protestant seminary in Cluj in the capitalist times, says that he has been sent by the party there to prepare the students in the radical sense.

When the Communists came to power in Rumania, Orthodox priests, Riosheanu, Patrashcoiu, and others, appeared dressed at once as colonels of the secret police and arrested and beat their parishioners. When the parishioners asked them, "But how is this possible? This is a nightmare. You have been my priest; I kissed your hand; I took the sacraments from you," they answered: "You dupes, you idiots, the Communist Party has sent us in the church."

We have surely had an infiltration. I have given you names, and we had it not only in the church, we had it in our state authorities, too. We had no FBI, but we had a Minister of Interior Affairs, something like your Hoover. His name was Ghelmegeanu.

When the Communists came to power, every policeman of the anti-Communist times was put in prison and tortured. He who had been the head of the police became a great man with the Communists. And they said, "He has been our man since long."

Surely they use this infiltration. Now I am not interested in politics, but I wonder about churches. Jesus has said it so clearly, "Beware of wolves dressed in sheepskins." And now I have asked the church leaders, "You are my leader, I am a very little and insignificant pastor. Wrongly, a halo has been created about around me just because I made 14 years of prison. But I know I am very insignificant, and I am below an average Christian. You are a church leader. Tell me, from what have I to beware? Who are these wolves dress in sheepskins?"

They couldn't tell me. These are Communists, and Communist fellow travelers who infiltrate in churches and everywhere and destroy especially the faith of the youths.

My son, who studies now psychology in California, is afraid about what he sees. He came from an anti-Communist university in Bucharest. I call it so because all the students in Rumania are anti-Communists. And here, he hears the praises of communism in the University of California at Los Angeles. Four Soviet motion pictures are shown every month, attended by the students. In Bucharest, Soviet motion pictures are boycotted. Nobody goes to look at them.

Americans don't permit trade with Red China. Now how do the books of Mao Tse-tung on which it is written "printed in Peking" arrive to America? They are sold in the University of California for a dollar apiece. And the students buy it. How does it arrive? Does no police see it?

Then my son wrote a letter to Reagan—my son is very young—and he said, "Mr. Reagan, I am the son of a pastor who has been 14 years in Communist prisons and I thought, as you, too, may be in a Communist prison very soon, to give you some information how a Communist prison is, and I will tell you why you will be in a Communist prison. If you will allow that the youth should be trained as it is trained here, with such motion pictures, with the books of Mao Tse-tung, and inscriptions on the walls, 'American murderers,' and all these things, then surely they will become Communists." And dear Reagan, or someone in his name, answered with a beautiful letter to my son, in which he thanked him and he says, "I know all these things. And I try myself to do the best against it." I quote from memory.

Horrible things are happening here. America is now my second fatherland. First of all, every man who loves freedom has two fatherlands, his own and America, because if America falls, then there is no hope for freedom for anybody in the world. Secondly, America is my home now. And I must say that my heart bleeds for America. My heart bleeds when I see this apathy towards the Communist menace.

Mr. SMITH. Did the Communists in your country incite racial hatred?

Mr. WURMBRAND. Oh, surely. The Communist Party of Rumania had in her program the right of self-determination of every province. In Rumania, we have many national minorities. We have the Hungarians, Bulgarians, and Turks. We have in Bessarabia Russians and Ukrainians. But we formed into one state, one nation. They said to the Transylvanians, you should secede from Rumania, and you, the Bessarabians, should secede, and to others, you should secede. And there have been rebellions organized by them.

For example, in Bessarabia, they profited of some justified dissatisfactions which always exist and incited this hatred. They organized a bloody riot in Tatar-Bunar. Some of the national minorities believed them. The Communists came to power. Then something very interesting happened. I was in the prison of Tirgul-Ocna, and the commandant of the prison told me, "Now, Mr. Wurmbrand, you see, you have suffered under the Nazis. The Nazis were so bad and persecuted the Jews. We are not like this. Just look around you in the prison. You have in prison Rumanians, Hungarians, Russians, Jews, we put everybody in prison. We make no racial difference."

Here in America, you may have racial dissatisfactions, riots, and difference. When the Communists will come to power, Mr. Brown and Mr. Carmichael and their white opponents and the fighters for civil rights will be together in the same prison. There will be a full integration, I promise you. There will be no black power, nor white power. There will be dictatorship over black and white.

Mr. SMITH. Are there any American citizens being detained by force in Rumania at the present time?

Mr. WURMBRAND. Yes. After my information, something like 40–50 American citizens, American-born, are hindered to leave Rumania. I have given the names to the State Department through Senators and Congressmen. I have received also the answer. Many interventions have been made by the State Department and by the American Embassy in Bucharest to allow them to leave the country. They are not allowed to leave. Ask yourself why were they not allowed to leave, when I was allowed, although I had not the American state behind me.

Mr. SMITH. Why are they being detained?

Mr. WURMBRAND. Why are they being detained? I can tell you what they wished in my case and in the case of the Jews they sold. They wish money. It is generally known that they have made slave trade with Jews. The one who took the money was Corneliu Manescu, a Jewish Communist, but an anti-Semite, a traitor to his own race. He is our [Rumania's] Secretary of State [Foreign Minister]. This slave trader will be, with the vote of U.S.A., president of the next Assembly of the organization of United Nations.

Mr. SMITH. You mean, they are holding these people for ransom?

Mr. WURMBRAND. The precedent with the Jews makes me believe this.

And now what I wonder very much about is that Americans are selling now a steel mill to Rumania. I read, I could not check it, that you are giving to Rumania enriched uranium, too. You help Fiat make a car plant there.

Now, if the Americans would say, "I give you a steel mill. I give you something, you give me also something. You need badly the steel mill. Give me my 50 citizens." They would have them immediately.

With a gangster, you can't speak in another manner. The American citizens could very easily be obtained if this condition would be put. I have seen bridges built. I have spoken to the engineers. Bridges are always built from two sides. You can't build a bridge from one side. I keep your citizen here by force and you build a bridge towards me and give me money. I never speak politics. But I have to put a question. I hear Rumania gets a car plant, so Russia. Communist countries get loans and many goods. The same countries say that they support North Vietnam against Americans. In the end it appears that American boys are killed with American dollars. That is my impression. But I don't speak out on politics. I just happened to think of it.

Mr. SMITH. Are these American people charged with any crime or given any reason for this detention?

Mr. WURMBRAND. No. They are American-born citizens. They have lived long in Rumania and Rumania does not acknowledge their American citizenship, although they are Americans just like you.

Mr. SMITH. Two of the principal foreign proponents of a dialogue between Communists and Christians are Josef Hromadka of Czechoslovakia and Roger Garaudy of France, whom we have previously mentioned.

Mr. WURMBRAND. Yes.

Mr. SMITH. Both of these men have been recently in the United States lecturing at many universities on the merits and necessity of a dialogue between Communists and Christians. What is your opinion of their activities in this respect? Is it deceptive?

Mr. WURMBRAND. I have promised to myself in witnessing to give no opinions, but only facts. On the 10th of July there was a convention of the Lutheran Church, Missouri Synod. It was attended by Dr. Mihalko, chairman of the Commission on Worship and Spiritual Life of the Lutheran World Federation. He is a Czechoslovankian. This man declared previously in a dialogue, "Socialism represents high moral values and pursues honestly humanistic goals. Socialism has not liquidated the church and has not persecuted it."

And then again, "It has not misused the church for its purposes."

Mihalko asserted that socialism has not persecuted the church. Then Kosygin and Brezhnev are liars, because they say in the Soviet press, "We persecute the church." They say, "We have created the atheistic school of the irreconcilable." They say, "We have taken away children from their mothers only because they are Christians." And Mihalko, Hromadka, and Nikodim come to tell us that there is no persecution. Niemoeller has been here, the vice chairman of the World Council of Churches. I happened to be in Norway at the same time with him. He came to Norway, having a schedule to preach. On the first day he said in an interview that communism has made no martyrs more since 1920. I answered in the press, asking Niemoeller: "Have you ever heard about Cardinal Mindszenty? Was he arrested before or after 1920? Have you ever heard about Cardinal Beran? Have you not heard about Eastern German Protestant pastors, pastors of your fatherland, arrested after 1920? Why do you lie?" Then the newspaper called him and said, "You have at your disposal our columns to answer to Wurmbrand." He said, "I have no time." And, though scheduled to preach in Norway, he simply fled.

They have no answers. The facts can't be contradicted. I can be contradicted. About me they can say whatever they like. I will never answer them. I acknowledge beforehand that they may be better men than I am. But their "facts" are lies. Hromadka went to see Mikoyan. Now usually, it is said that Stalin has committed crimes. Who has been his henchmen? Mikoyan has been the right hand of Stalin and Khrushchev and Brezhnev and Kosygin.

Now you have before you Mikoyan or Podgorny, and you are a Christian. I would also talk with Mikoyan and would tell him to repent of his crimes and to become a Christian, but they just smiled at each other, congratulated each other for peace, and so on.

I can't admit that the Hromadkas are Christians. I can't accept them. May God forgive them. May God recognize them as Christians; I can't recognize the one who trods on the blood of martyrs.

Mr. SMITH. Reverend Wurmbrand, do you have any information as to the attitudes of Russian and Rumanian immigrants in this country respecting the Communist regime's persecution of religion in their own countries?

Mr. WURMBRAND. Well, most of the immigrants are surely patriots and they love their country of origin and they have the Christian point of view. There are some who try to compromise with the Communist government. These have very interesting experiences.

I have here a declaration which I will depose in the file, by a Rumanian, Theodorescu from Detroit. He saith in his declaration, "I was attracted by what I was told, that there everything has mellowed, and so on, so I wished to go back to Rumania and I presented myself to the Rumanian Embassy. The Rumanian Embassy said, 'Oh, if you wish to go back that is perfectly all right, but you must prove to us your loyalty first. And you must prove it in three manners:

"'First of all, go to Munich and spy out who are the Rumanians who give information to Radio Free Europe. Secondly, you will go to Yugoslavia and will find out what Rumanian groups transport anti-Communist literature. You must find Jon Chirila, an anti-Communist who attacked the legation in Bern in '55, and either you must kidnap him or you must kill him, and then we will accept you.' "

Whatever Rumanian or Russian or so enters in relationship with Communist consulates has the same experience. I have been in prison with several repatriated emigrants. I recall one, the Colonel Baiulescu, who has been an emigrant and who had believed the stories about mellowing. He came back to Rumania, I swear before God that I tell you exactly the fact as it happened. He had been a major in the royal army. When he came back, they gave him the uniform of a colonel; they photographed him as such and they put the picture in the Rumanian newspaper. They sent him from place to place to deliver lectures about how bad it is in the West and how happy he is to be now in a Communist country. And after he has delivered all these lectures, he got 20 years of prison.

Mr. TUCK. The House of Representatives is now in session, and we will have to terminate this hearing pretty quickly. I understand that you probably have a closing statement that you would like to make.

Mr. WURMBRAND. Yes; a closing statement of just a few minutes.

I have many other facts about the persecution in Byelorussia, in Lithuania. In Albania, they have closed all the churches. In Red China, there exists not one church. In Cuba, they take out first blood of those executed, and so on, but I will leave all these things. I wish to make just a last statement.

I know that the Communists will react very violently against what I have done today. They have threatened me before I left Rumania and they have their friends here; they have their friends even in the churches. They will say many bad things about me. I acknowledge beforehand that all the evil which they will say about me is true.

I don't wish to appear as self-righteous. I am not a better man than the Communists. I have been from youth an anarchical element. I have been brought up without any religion and until the age of 27 I hated all those whom the Communist hate. I admired Lenin and Marx just for one thing, for being atheists and I gladly would have suffered for atheism. But I hated Communists, too. I hated everybody. I have had a very bitter youth, and this has produced in me this. So that anybody can say about me whatever they like, and it will be true. Only the blood of Christ washed my sins and cured me from hatred, putting love instead, even love towards the Communists as men.

Since I am a Christian, I have been a very weak Christian. I have also committed many sins of a Christian being. I have not arrived to be a saint. So they can attack me, and I will never answer to any personal attack, but will say always, "You have said less sins about me than these which I have really committed."

But nobody in the world can deny what I say about the persecution of Christians and Jews happening today. Nobody in the world! They may say about Wurmbrand whatever they like. I will not even answer them. My answer is these facts. I answer with the blood of the martyrs which cries like the blood of Abel. God will ask the church leaders who compromise with communism: "Cain, where is your brother, Abel?" The facts presented by me can't be contradicted.

Let the members of the Communist Party, let the clergymen who believe that there is liberty in the Soviet camp, let them write to me, and I will give them other facts.

I have published now a book *Today's Martyred Church, Tortured for Christ*.

A second book, *Wurmbrand's Letters*, will appear next week. A book, published by Coward McCann, *Christ in Communist Prisons*, will also appear soon and will give new facts.

I defy any political leader who says that communism has softened and mellowed to contradict these facts of '66 and '67, which I have brought.

Just a minute more. I assert that never has the persecution in the Communist camp been so bad as now. Two-thirds of the Communist camp is Red China. Never in the whole history of communism have ministers been buried alive as it happened in Ten Sheen now. Never in the history of communism have all the churches of a country been closed as it happened now in Red China and in Albania.

I didn't arrive to speak to you about Bulgaria or Poland, and so on. Communism rules one-third of the world. I spoke to you about the suffering of one-third of the world. One-third of the world should be one-third of your religious services, one-third of your prayers, one-third of your gifts, one-third of your concerns, one-third of your sermons.

Allow me to tell you that in Communist prisons, I have seen prisoners with 50-pound chains at their feet, praying for America and for its churches. Every night we prayed, and now I go from church to church in America and seldom I hear even a prayer or a mentioning of those who have 50-pound chains at their feet, because they fight for God, for liberty, and for the preservation of America, too. And therefore I appeal to all the churches to rank-and-file church members and to leaders, I appeal to patriotic organizations to publish these facts and all the other facts which they can find in my books, which they can have simply by writing to me at Post Office Box 11, Glendale, California 91209. I ask them to arrange public protests. There have been hundreds of clergymen who have protested against the war in Vietnam, but against killing of Christians there have been no picketing, no public protests. I ask them to organize this. I don't ask them to send support to the organization to which I belong, but make it that your church should help families of Christian martyrs, should help the underground church with Bibles. There should be a prayer campaign. No church service in which the martyrs are not mentioned is valid before God.

I forgot in prison the Lord's Prayer. We were doped. My mind was destroyed. I couldn't say an "Our Father." We needed your prayers. The underground church is the only organized resistance against communism and it should have the help of the Christians and of the patriots of America.

I thank the committee very much, because it gave me this possibility to show all these facts. I value this commission very much. I wonder about one thing. I sought in Los Angeles and in Washington from one bookshop to another the records of the hearings of this committee and couldn't find them in bookshops. But these facts should be largely published and so we should stop the hands of the murderers of Christians and of Jews, because I love the Christians, I love the Jews, and I love the murderers, too. My last word should be about a Jew, the rabbi of Lyubavich. When the police agents of the Communists pointed a gun at him, they said, "This little toy has made many a man change his mind." And the rabbi of Lyubavich calmly replied, "This little toy can intimidate only that kind of man who has many gods, his passions, and but one world, this world; but I have only one God and two worlds. I am not impressed by this little toy."

Neither is the Christian church impressed by all the terror of the Communists. Christ will be the victor in the Communist camp, too.

I thank you very much.

God bless you!

Mr. Tuck. We thank you very much for your most interesting and informative testimony. As chairman of the subcommittee, I would like to say that I wish that every man and woman in America could hear what you have to say.

Mr. Roudebush. I want to also join in complimenting the reverend for coming before our committee and giving excellent testimony.

I am delighted that you did give us this information so we can print it and place it in the hands of the Congress and the public.

Mr. Wurmbrand. God bless you and God bless America!

Mr. Tuck. The subcommittee will stand in recess until called together again by the chairman.

(Whereupon, at 12:45 p.m., Thursday, August 10, 1967, the subcommittee adjourned, to reconvene at the call of the Chair.)

The author welcomes correspondence.

Enquiries and gifts for the Underground Church may be sent to

JESUS TO THE COMMUNIST WORLD, INC.

P.O. Box 2947, Torrance, CA 90509

WURMBRAND
WORLDWIDE
BEST SELLERS

CHRIST ON THE JEWISH ROAD

by Rev. Richard Wurmbrand

Rev. Richard Wurmbrand narrates his experiences as a missionary to the Jews before the Communist takeover of Romania. "The fate of a farmer in Vietnam, who has never seen a Jew in his life, will, in the last resort, depend on whether he reads the book about the Jew Jesus (The Bible) or the book about the Jew Marx (The Communist Manifesto)."

4¾" x 7"   190 pages

4 oz. paperback $3.95   **HODDER**

_____ _____

IN GOD'S UNDERGROUND

by Rev. Richard Wurmbrand

"Unless the permissive age has died completely to a sense of the miraculous, his story can hardly fail to be a world sensation." *Evening News* (London) "I have decided to give to every priest in my diocese a copy of your book!" – The Late Archbishop Fulton J. Sheen.

4¼" x 7"   254 pages   **DIANE BOOKS**

6.5 oz. paperback $2.75

_____ _____

VICTORIOUS FAITH

By Rev. Richard Wurmbrand

A collection of Christian meditations. Are you confronted by the terrible fact of suffering? This book will give you light! "Only one who has been as close to the Flaming Heart of Christ could ever send so many sparks to the readers," – The Late Archbishop Fulton J. Sheen.

4¼" x 7"   128 pages   **DIANE BOOKS**

6.5 oz. paperback $3.95

_____ _____

TORTURED FOR CHRIST

by Rev. Richard Wurmbrand

Months of solitary confinement, years of periodic physical torture, constant suffering from hunger and cold, the anguish of brainwashing and mental cruelty – experienced and witnessed by Rev. Richard Wurmbrand, a Romanian minister, during his fourteen years in Communist prisons. An account of the suffering of the Undergound Church in countries behind the Iron Curtain. Torn from their loved ones, battered and beaten in body but not in spirit, they continue undaunted, in their Christian faith. More than 3,000,000 copies sold!

4¼" x 7"   144 pages   **DIANE BOOKS**

3 oz. paperback $1.75

_____ _____

WAS KARL MARX A SATANIST?

by Rev. Richard Wurmbrand

Was Karl Marx a devil worshipper? Were hymns of praise to devil sung in his home? Some of the extensive scientific evidence presented in this book will startle you!

4¼" x 7"   96 pages   **DIANE BOOKS**

3 oz. paperback $2.00

_____ _____

CONTINUED NEXT PAGE!

WURMBRAND
WORLDWIDE
BEST SELLERS

IF IT WERE CHRIST, WOULD YOU GIVE HIM YOUR BLANKET?

by Rev. Richard Wurmbrand

"Two Chinese Christians shivered with cold in a cell. Each had a thin blanket. One of the Christians looked to the other and saw how he trembled. The thought came to him, 'If that were Christ, would you give him your blanket?' Of course he would. Immediately he spread the blanket over his brother."

4¼" x 7"   128 pages   **DIANE BOOKS**
4.5 oz. paperback $1.75

_____ _____

WITH GOD IN SOLITARY CONFINEMENT

by Rev. Richard Wurmbrand

"This is a most astonishing, perhaps the most astonishing book that I have read. Richard Wurmbrand must surely be one of the most remarkable Christians living today." — J.B. Phillips, Translator of the New Testament.

A collection of sermons "to the angels" composed by Rev. Richard Wurmbrand during his 2½ years spent in solitary confinement.

4¼" x 7"   192 pages   **DIANE BOOKS**
4 oz. paperback $3.95

_____ _____

THE ANSWER TO MOSCOW'S BIBLE

by Rev. Richard Wurmbrand

This book is the Christian answer to the famous Atheist's Handbook widely spread and studied through the entire Communist world. The Soviet press admitted this book of Rev. Richard Wurmbrand to be the most influential and damaging book to Communist propaganda.

5¼" x 8"   192 pages   **HODDER**
4.2 oz. paperback $3.95

_____ _____

ORDER FORM

Prices subject to change without notice.

Minimum Order: $5.00

Subtotal _____
In California add tax 6% _____
Minimum handling ____1.00____
Plus Postage: 12% of total _____
Total _____

SHIP TO:

Name _____

Street Address _____

City _____ State _____ Zip _____

DIANE BOOKS, P.O. BOX 2948, TORRANCE, CALIFORNIA 90509, USA

PLEASE ENCLOSE PAYMENT WITH ORDER!

INDEX

INDIVIDUALS

ORGANIZATIONS

A

B

C

E

F

H

I

L

M

N

R

U

W

PUBLICATIONS

D

H

J

P

T

○